CREATING THE NEW
INTERNET SUPER HIGHWAY

CREATING THE NEW

INTERNET SUPER HIGHWAY

Taking the Web to another Dimension

Written by

Alastair R Agutter

CREATING THE NEW

INTERNET SUPER HIGHWAY

"Taking the Web to another Dimension"

BY ALASTAIR R AGUTTER

First Recorded and Published 15th May 2015.

Printed, Published and Distributed by

Create Space Independent Publishing

An Amazon Group Company

ISBN-10: 1512231169

ISBN-13: 978-1512231168

CONTENTS

"A Completely New Way of Thinking Surrounding the World Wide Web in the 21st Century"

QUOTATION

"Even a virtual world created by technology, continues to be re-shaped by the power of Natural Law in the form of Quantum Mechanics and Natural Branching."

~ Alastair R Agutter

TO MY READERS

"Please forgive me for my warped sense of humour regarding the illustration examples throughout the book. But in my defence, I think Science and Technology should be a platform of fun learning, not watching paint dry."

Best Wishes, Alastair ☺

Introduction!

Firstly, I would like to thank you for acquiring a copy of this book "Creating the New Internet Super Highway" for an insight now surrounding the future landscape of the World Wide Web and the ability to deploy new technologies now and in the future for the 21st Century!

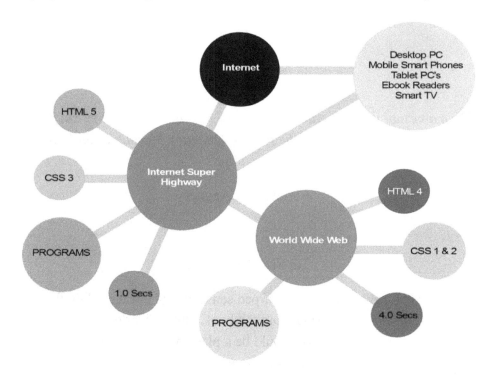

Created and Designed by Alastair R Agutter 2013

This book provides proven information on taking any participant party involved with the World Wide Web to a whole new dimension and different level of thinking.

So let's start with some basics!

The Commercial World Wide Web as we know it began in 1994, with the development of browser software namely Mosaic created by Marc Andreessen and Eric Bina while at NCSA, Champagne, Illinois, USA.

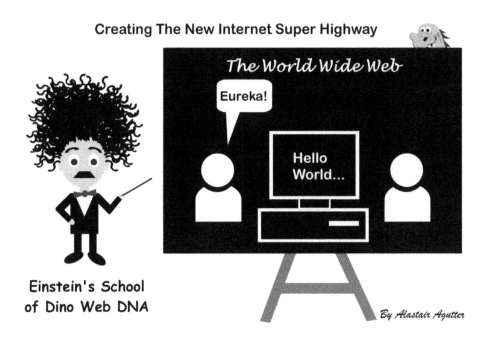

My participation surrounding the World Wide Web began as a UK founding Netscape DevEdge Member developing and customizing Netscape Navigator Software Browser Suites in the mid 90's, some 21 plus years ago as a Senior WWW Developer. A period I described as early hazy days, consisting of students, enthusiasts and academics.

In just over two decades the landscape of the World Wide Web has dramatically changed in relation to hardware, connectivity and software, regarding user participation for education, products and services, as most of the world today is now connected to the World Wide Web in some form.

From a few 10's of thousands of users in the mid 90's, today there are over 2 billion web users. As a result of such changes, you do not have to be a mathematical genius or rocket scientist to realise the user demand is significantly different.

In the early days of poor connectivity with 28k and 56k modems, any form of access to documentation or pictures when visiting a web site, was a great achievement in itself. But those days of the web enthusiast has sadly gone and been replaced today with a cyber world of continued advancements, greater social interaction, daily commerce trading, online banking to IRS Government Tax returns.

The realization of such a diverse traffic environment of demands today could never be retained or maintained in the same existing framework and as like all of Natural Law surrounding Quantum Mechanics and Natural Branching things have to change!

Alastair R Agutter

QUOTATION

"If the spirit of your imagination is limited, your journey of discovery will be very short."

~ Alastair R Agutter

In The Beginning

Today we can readily acknowledge from technology advancements a virtual world in addition to a physical one does now exist!

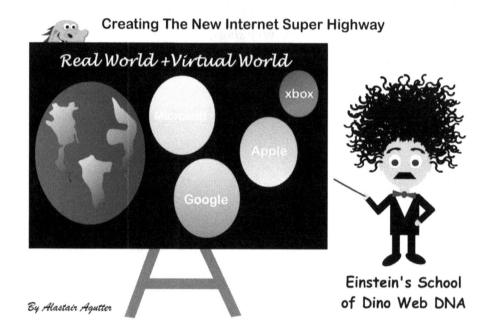

Creating The New Internet Super Highway

Real World + Virtual World

xbox
Microsoft
Apple
Google

By Alastair Agutter

Einstein's School
of Dino Web DNA

The fascinating factor in all that we can learn from this book is the power of Sir Isaac Newton's Natural Law, where such rules also apply in a virtual world as well as in a real world.

As a Senior WWW Developer and Programmer, now for over 21 years I have always been at the forefront of writing the technology story surrounding the World Wide Web with other partners and by fully understanding the geographical landscape, one can see the evolving changes taking place now and in the near future that serves to assist me in determining what is required!

Regarding what is required, any developer I believe attuned to such an environment can always produce a vast shopping list for change. But the starting point in any advancement and especially surrounding communication is the constraints placed upon us surrounding the technology of the day!

Natural Law consistently teaches us the need for understanding balance in all that we do, for within Natural Law in the realms of Quantum Mechanics, there are two key essential ruling functions and these are to "Evolve and Refine". However, regarding us the human race, very often like Children or adolescents, we very often tend to become drunk from the excesses of something (new gadget or product) and this can become a problem!

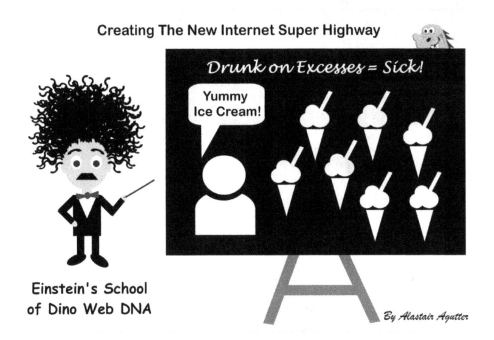

From Social Networking to Multiple Devices, from hardware storage to cloud data gathering, from valve television to transistor Smart TV, when such technologies are born and arrive in our commercial consumer driven world, the human race can become very quickly and easily drawn in and consumed by such advancements.

As a species evolving, the human race in a short period of time has had a significant impact on the environment. Early days of local and regional evolution did not impede or impact the community at large, only the localities the human race inhabited at that time!

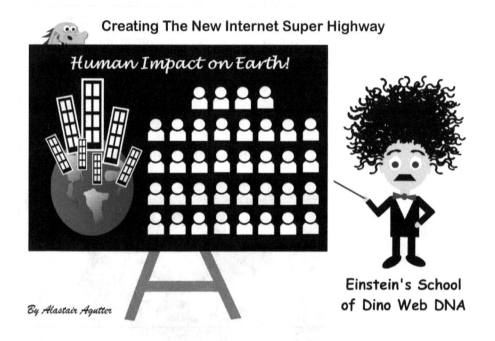

Creating The New Internet Super Highway

Human Impact on Earth!

By Alastair Agutter

Einstein's School of Dino Web DNA

However today, with a population of over 7 billion human beings on Earth and an interconnected community, the consequences and impact of our actions is now very noticeable, especially surrounding Climate Change.

As we continue to advance as a human race and up the stakes in technology and science, the window of allowance for error is forever becoming smaller.

So every step we now take forward today comes with very serious consequence!

Throughout history prior to the 21st century the human race has essentially quantified and departmentalized in 1D and 2D patterns, this can be seen in the emergence of computing technology operating in a binary environment of 1's and 0's.

As we advance more from this point we are beginning to apply different thought processes, these including 3D concepts and multiple facets from studying Quantum Mechanics and Fractal Maths.

We are also aware today of fractal maths and where from such understanding, mathematical calculus can vary in different dimensions and frameworks that are in play in relation to volume, linear, symmetry and time.

The concept and application of computer coding as mentioned above is currently binary, but this will be changing soon as we come to understand more about how everything works and functions, especially when we drill down and begin to discover and understand how particle matter forms and functions and with far more complex variants almost beyond human comprehension. However, as more is discovered in relation to the DNA gene code sequence of particle matter as I call it, such an environment of learning and knowledge will become more fundamental and a norm in science and bio-chemistry discovery.

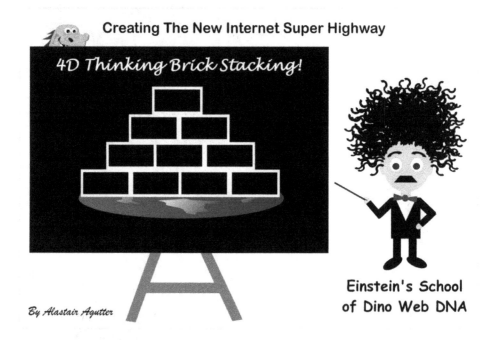

Creating The New Internet Super Highway

4D *Thinking Brick Stacking!*

By Alastair Agutter

Einstein's School
of Dino Web DNA

At this time Computer Science is exploring countless avenues, one being Tesseract a four dimensional concept I describe as "Brick Stacking" in an effort to utilize volume and space, where key rules always apply in Natural Law, where Quantum Mechanics is always applying the rules to "Evolve and Refine" and such concepts, or laws can be seen across all of our everyday lives in the advancement of all products created by Man and all life entities on Earth and in fact beyond, in the Cosmos!

The discovering and creating of "The New Internet Super Highway" has been from considering a Virtual World rather than a Physical World. The

Internet first began its journey when it was operated as ARPANET (Advanced Research Projects Agency Network) and funded by the United States of America Department of Defence, using packet data and TCIP protocols. The concept discovered, considered and formulated in October of 1963 by Computer Scientists J.C.R Licklider of Bolt, Berenak and Newman. Such an environment was the precursor to what we know today as the internet.

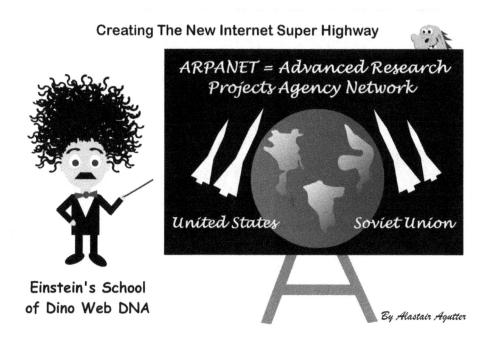

Both technologies the ARPANET and the INTERNET were developed and created in a physical world environment. Whereas the discovery and creation of "The New Internet Super Highway", has been born from applying logic and thought to a Virtual World and beyond a one and two dimensional thought process.

As I mentioned earlier, Computing today regarding the development and creation of data and programs derives from applying "Alpha Numeric's" ones and twos.

In the following picture is an example of how Computing will change and start using a new coding known as "Symommetry" a more advanced coding process than Alpha Numeric's of ones and twos. This will be the first time you have been introduced to "Symommetry" for it is a name I have created to define this new coding structure with six elements plus and beyond 1 and 2 dimensional thinking!

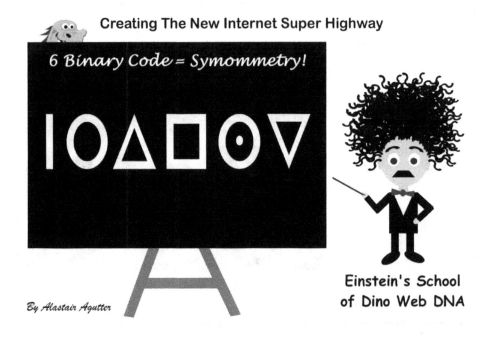

Symommetry can be described as a quantum leap in thinking surrounding the Computer Sciences, for "Symommetry" is dimensional as a coding process, unlike "Alpha Numeric's" which is linear. Symommetry can take programming to a more sophisticated multi-faceted level and reaching beyond 1 and 2 dimensional thinking or processing.

As Scientists now continue to explore and try to understand and discover the "Higgs-Boson" today known as the "God" particle. I think the best way to describe "Symommetry" as a new dimensional code is in a similar form. For with this form of new programming we are going to go beyond 1 and 2 elements to a configuration of 6 elements plus and as a result in a linear sense, programming can be expanded from 1 and 2 elements to 6 plus elements. However, as we explore Natural Law in the form of encompassing both Natural Branching and Quantum Mechanics the opportunities are boundless by introducing 6 plus elements as this form of programming will be able to translate into data form particle and sub atomic particle matter configurations and elements. This will be required!

As we begin to understand particle matter more and how each element functions surrounding how particles form and vibrate from harmonics to create smells and objects for example, such a programming will be required.

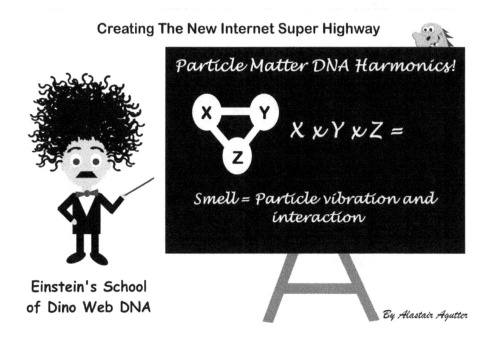

Creating The New Internet Super Highway

Particle Matter DNA Harmonics!

$X \times Y \times Z =$

Smell = Particle vibration and interaction

Einstein's School of Dino Web DNA

By Alastair Agutter

Natural Law in the form of Quantum Mechanics and Natural Branching does not function by measurement alone, or functions in a linear thought process.

The World Wide Web is a replication today of how Natural Law in the form of Natural Branching works by one computer connected to another and another and another. And within this environment data documents and images exist on one computer, connected to another and another and another.

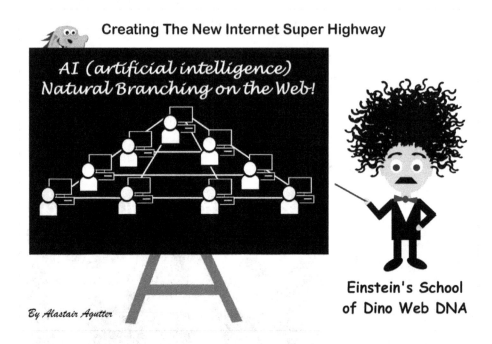

Creating The New Internet Super Highway

AI (artificial intelligence) Natural Branching on the Web!

By Alastair Agutter

Einstein's School of Dino Web DNA

The documents themselves are also connected from one document to another and another and another. The same is the case in programming and operating systems and more recently open source development applications.

So as you can see the measurement or the function of such an environment is not moving in a linear sense from one point to another and measuring time and distance! For in the World of Quantum Mechanics and Natural Branching such values can exist but amongst countless others that are 1, 2, 3 and 4 plus and even 5th dimensional.

The following image gives a precise example of the many facets of Computing with one PC holding ever increasing larger masses of data and then connecting to the web, to join other computers also storing various forms of data. What can be concluded from such facts is, there exists mass naturally branching and on an ever increasing size every day!

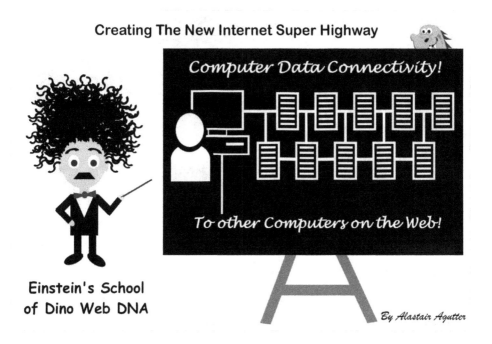

Creating The New Internet Super Highway

Computer Data Connectivity!

To other Computers on the Web!

Einstein's School
of Dino Web DNA

By Alastair Agutter

Albert Einstein after 20 years of research into Quantum Mechanics got it! He wanted to be able to achieve a mathematical calculation of these events surrounding Quantum Mechanics to be able to departmentalize or quantify such events to accommodate the human thought process at the time. Therefore what was required was an explanation and understanding for the Science and Physics community especially. However, as I say, after Albert Einstein's 20 years of research and dedication into Quantum Mechanics, he did in fact get it saying "God has a sense of humour."

In fairness to Albert Einstein who I deeply admire and have a great affinity and affection towards, He did get it and even the calculation of Quantum Mechanics, when referring to "God's sense of humour."

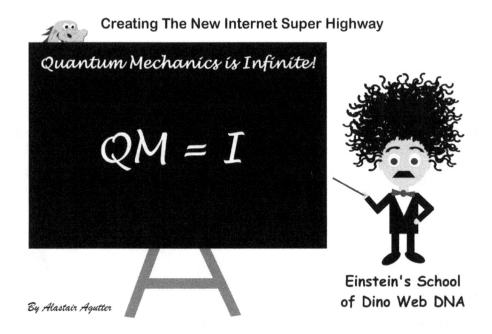

Creating The New Internet Super Highway

Quantum Mechanics is Infinite!

$$QM = I$$

By Alastair Agutter

Einstein's School of Dino Web DNA

You see the answer and calculation to Quantum Mechanics is "Infinite!"

$QM = I$

You see in the measurement and calculation of Quantum Mechanics the equation can add up to whatever you want. For in Quantum Mechanics all and everything is possible.

Hence my measured definition of the calculation Albert derived at which was 0 as he could not quantify what we would describe as a phenomena. So the calculation of Quantum Mechanics is in effect $QM = I = 0$?

QM = Quantum Mechanics

I = Infinite

Definition of Infinite:-

"Unlimited or unmeasurable in extent of space, duration of time, etc. the infinite nature of outer space, Unbounded or unlimited, boundless, endless."

So the Quantum Mechanics calculation of what Quantum Mechanics is and how it can be measured equals "it can be anything and everything" and this calculation is also connected to Natural Branching in relation to what needs to be done in a full cycle and therefore back to the Quantum Mechanics Covenant to "evolve and refine."

Quantum Mechanics will and can organically evolve and change as required in conjunction with its partner Natural Branching and will alter continuously regarding the environmental conditions of the time and this is where it gets interesting, as such facts can also encapsulate Charles Darwin's work surrounding the evolution of the species. For time will vary also at any time, any moment, or at any event if each one is different, leading always to a different calculation and measurement, but all calculations are in fact correct at the time of such an event is recorded and this encompasses motion that Albert Einstein was working on.

Quantum Mechanics equals Infinite, equalling "it can be anything and everything!"

Here below is a simple example of what I mean.

If I am at a fair ground and standing watching a Carousel going round with horses going up and down with people. If I record what I see every 15 minutes at that immediate time, the calculation of what I saw would be accurate and correct, but every recording would be different in relation to time, motion and spectrum of sight.

With regards to Sir Isaac Newton's Natural Law encompassing the realms of Quantum Mechanics and Natural Branching throws up directly into our face another key element and one that is also related to our limited knowledge of the "Big Bang."

You see one of the problems with reference to the human condition of one dimensional thinking in the Science and Physics community, is the way we try to understand many events and phenomena's and where very sadly we always try to bring it down to its most basic form and this relates to our progress and level of understanding regarding the Sciences.

Let me explain with "The Big Bang" as one prime example. The Science and Physics community are applying their knowledge to explain the "Big Bang Theory" based on factual knowledge of the events they know at that time in human evolutionary knowledge. This following example being regarding the Big Bang, where in simple terms, there has been a reactive explosion of matter and from that explosion gases and particles, which have sped out in all directions from one such event. So the Science and Physics community are applying knowledge based on factual events for further answers.

What the Science and Physics community are missing, is that they should be applying a reverse pattern of thinking by asking from such an event, what were the conditions that caused the Big Bang to happen. By applying that methodology they would then conclude as written in my book, where my work has been recorded in a publication titled "The Theory of Particle Matter Frequencies and Multiple Universes" discussing how another element does in fact exist that relates to the Big Bang, Quantum Mechanics and Natural Branching! In fact all three topics contain a common denominator element that is also connected and related and the same said element I believe will be proved to be Peter Higgs Boson, but in the form of a data energy. In other words "Intelligence" and in sub atomic particle energy form at this time the human race is only aware of four general sectors and only at an infant stage just beginning to understand these which are 1/. The Strong Force, 2/. The Weak Force, 3/. Electromagnetic Force and 4/. The Gravitational Force. However regarding the latter, the 4th mentioned element category here referred and acknowledged by the Science community, believe this such force is determined by influence regarding object elements present in the cosmos and within relative close distance of each other e.g. Sun gravitational effects to planetary movements in relation to Earth and Moon gravity movement etc. However Gravitational Waves do exist and they can carry energy elements across a Universe and can have an impact even many millions of light years away.

This therefore convinces me even more, that the whole Universe and Universes vibrate (harmonics) from particle atoms that form everything and from such interaction creates energy and when presented with energy, you have a mechanism for exercising and storing intelligence.

There is further evidence to back up these statements, just recently in fact LIGO (The Laser Interferometer Gravitational-Wave Observatory) has now discovered gravitational waves throughout the universe as a result of events (intelligence) in the Cosmos and again mentioned in my book "The Theory of Particle Matter Frequencies and Multiple Universes," where I describe these Universes as seas of data (intelligence strings and nodes).

For it is a fact, for all the events and cycles to happen there must be the existence of an intelligence signature within particle matter and sub atomic atoms. In fact all that we know and all that exists in whatever form and however it may comprise has a collection of particles, and has to be driven by an intelligence force, as there is always consistent cycles.

This is now where we move onto the "Eureka Moment" and creation of "Creating The New Internet Super Highway" using a virtual world architecture and an entirely different method of thinking and considering how data can be changed that comprises of variable forms as is seen in Sir Isaac Newton's Natural Law, encompassing Quantum Mechanics and

23

Natural Branching in relation to Computers and Packet Data that that form the World Wide Web or Internet as often described.

QUOTATION

"Sometimes history can be made when searching for something else and then finding something different that is related."

~ Alastair R Agutter

THE EUREKA MOMENT

It was in many respects by chance that the following events came about, but then in saying that. If we continue to search long enough, we will come across much more than we ever sought.

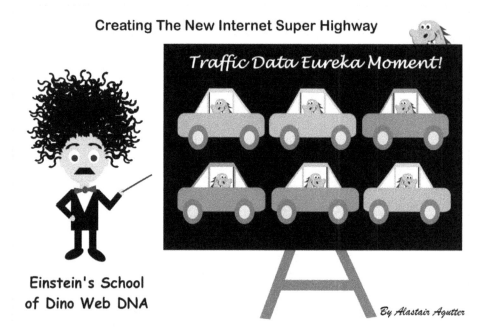

It was about May of 2013 that I began to check the Organization's web sites for traffic data, to get an idea on the amount of web visitors and areas of interest on Riverside Internationally.

Whilst carrying out such a process using some of my partners and friends technology at Google and Microsoft, I started to drill down on the data and came across the "Bounce Rate" metrics and data of the Organization's web sites. This information allowed me to travel across borders and look at every Country and Region World-Wide.

Even from smart efficient design, I discovered the average bounce rate for every one of our web sites was on average of around 40.6% and this horrified me!

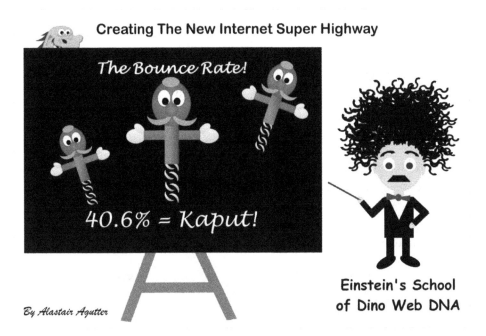

I know many of my readers who are Computer Scientists and Academics will understand what a bounce rate is! But for folk reading this information for the very first time and not familiar with this terminology and environment, I will further explain.

The Bounce Rate is the successful connection ratio to your web site by web user visitors. The bounce rate I mentioned above of 40.6% in real terms meant. Every 1000 web visitors around the world trying to access one of our web sites successfully, 406 could not connect and were unsuccessful. Leaving only 594 web users successfully gaining access!

That news is bad enough, but we have yet to determine the cause, or the time it was taking for every web user to connect to the web site.

In the previous introduction chapter, we began to discuss the realm of Natural Law and no doubt many readers would have been questioning this or asking why! But there is a great relevance, as I begin to explain where we consider the other factors and anomalies just surrounding the bounce rate.

From a 40.6% bounce rate, we are able to determined out of every 1000 web user connections to any web site, 406 web users are unsuccessful in making a connection and unable to view the web site landing (home) page.

So then you have to ask why?

You then have to consider the length of time it is taking for all 1000 web users to connect to the web site and why 406 web users could not connect successfully to the web site and how the other 594 could!

So what factors do we consider?

Connectivity speeds could be one consideration between Countries, but then you have to consider the size of the web site landing page itself in relation to data packet form and size. The actual device the web users are using is another consideration and the actual processing speed ability of the devices in question. By considering the aforementioned you can very quickly see and gather how the world of Natural Law is relevant in relation to Natural Branching and Quantum Mechanics surrounding even this subject area. The problem presented to us could be related to many numerous possibilities, facets and factors!

There are also other factors regarding this bounce rate conundrum in relation to Natural Branching and Quantum Mechanics, in relation to packet data flow and workarounds.

You see packet data travels at the speed of light and again does not operate or function in a linear form of thinking. E.g. getting from A to B in a traditional form of thinking pattern, as is the normal case with human beings.

As Human Beings we tend to determine getting from A to B is by the most direct route. But the World Wide Web as a vast expanding organic entity of artificial intelligence does not calculate in only 1 and 2 dimensional thought processes. Artificial Intelligence will utilize its full potential based on its functioning ability and capacity.

Very often when we are confronted with a problem as human beings, only then afterwards do we start the process of problem solving.

If for example we decide to plan a trip by road, the most direct route may not always be the most suitable solution. However we believe it should be! But if for example there are roadworks on our most direct route causing massive road and traffic delays, we may well consider another route based on the distance and time. Here regarding this process and thinking when presented with this dilemma creates moments of delay as human beings.

But in artificial intelligence terms, these thought processes are constant and where distance does not even bear any form of importance or priority. For the objective is to deliver the packet data by the most efficient and fastest way, regarding the delivery of the web sites landing page to the web user connecting to the web site address in question. So taking the road trip example here speed takes a priority over distance, interesting!

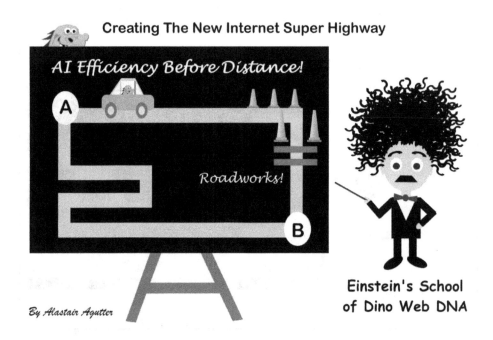

Creating The New Internet Super Highway

AI Efficiency Before Distance!

A

Roadworks!

B

By Alastair Agutter

Einstein's School of Dino Web DNA

Quantum Mechanics and Natural Branching is showing us even in a virtual world, how Natural Law functions with regards to the delivery and the efficiency of artificial intelligence that we would describe as "by the fastest means." Natural Law in the realm of Quantum Mechanics defines this as to "Evolve and Refine." It also demonstrates the rational and most logical calculated solution is not always the correct answer, or solution, therefore re-affirming the calculus of Quantum Mechanics does equal infinite. The example above is also demonstrating how the current laws of distance in relation to time can be changed as believed by Albert Einstein.

So as you can begin to see from one discovery of a Bounce Rate measurement, we have many elements to consider in this equation and ones that are not necessarily logical in the human thought pattern. Some may believe this explanation to be unnecessary and hard going, but all is of great importance in our evolution to be able to disseminate and drill down on microscopic issues that may well have a significant impact!

The more human's evolve, the smaller the window of error becomes as mentioned earlier and this is worth remembering, especially surrounding the world of computer sciences regarding artificial intelligence or Nuclear Fusion and Fission!

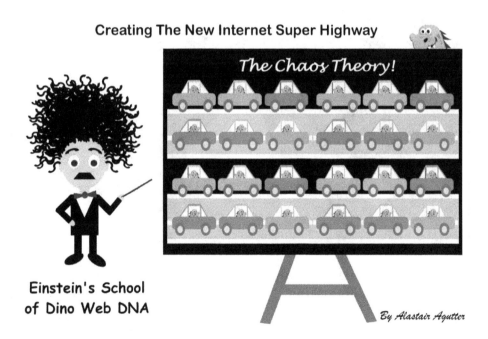

Creating The New Internet Super Highway

The Chaos Theory!

Einstein's School of Dino Web DNA

By Alastair Agutter

As I started to examine more closely the "Bounce Rate" of the web sites and considered the ever increasing number of users to the World Wide

Web for transporting all this information and the more being published by the second, a "Deja Vu" moment hit me surrounding a paper I wrote back in 2006. The paper concerned the World Wide Web and the paper was called "The Chaos Theory." I knew then at that moment in May of 2013, as I examined the data regarding the bounce rate, things had to change and something needed to be done!

I realized looking at the bigger picture how critical it was that the World Wide Web had to change and adopt the principles of Natural Law, especially in relation to Quantum Mechanics to "evolve and refine" to prevent continued blockages and meltdown across the World Wide Web, as it continued to Naturally Branch with more data and programs by the second, minute, hour and day etc.

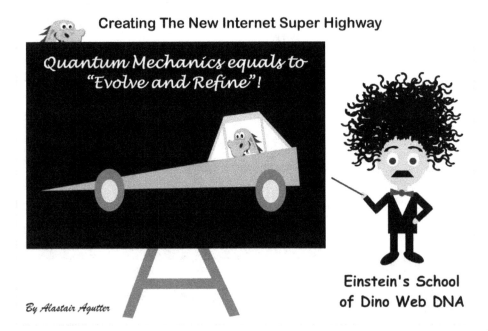

Creating The New Internet Super Highway

Quantum Mechanics equals to "Evolve and Refine"!

By Alastair Agutter

Einstein's School of Dino Web DNA

They say we all have a journey and path in life mapped out already and perhaps this is true! For it was from my experience when working as a Microsoft Channel Partner Developer on the WebTV platform project in conjunction with Phillips in the mid to late 1990's, it helped me to find a solution to this ever increasing problem looming regarding the World Wide Web. For in those early days of developing WebTV, the set top boxes developed by colleagues at Philips, had only a storage capacity of 15 megabytes. Within this small amount of storage, we had to put a channels visual and text program framework together. At the same time, we also had to allow enough storage for television users to bookmark and store their favourite channels and services.

Creating The New Internet Super Highway

Der Perfect Web Page!

Einstein's School
of Dino Web DNA

By Alastair Agutter

So regarding the Bounce Rate of the web sites, it really presented me with an opportunity to seek a solution to address the whole of the World Wide Web problem!

Funnily enough again, it was back to the past in years gone by, where I use to discuss "Great Web Design," and use to explain to web designers and developers the importance of ensuring their projects were accessible for every potential web user world-wide. I often described it as a cake of opportunity.

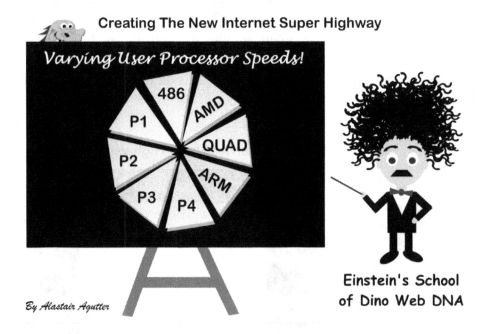

Creating The New Internet Super Highway

Varying User Processor Speeds!

486
AMD
P1
QUAD
P2
ARM
P3
P4

By Alastair Agutter

Einstein's School of Dino Web DNA

Here regarding the cake of opportunity, I explained from connectivity and processor speeds of PC's in those days, the more sophisticated a web site became the greater the risk of the web user audience being unable to access or process the medium designed and developed. As a result of the web user technology of the day and therefore removing large slices of your potential audience base. The bounce rate scenario was replicating the problems posed in those days back in the mid to late 90's!

So what could be done to address the organic growth of the World Wide Web in relation to many varying device types, data and programs?

As a founding Netscape DevEdge Member, customizing the Netscape Navigator Suite for UK consumer and business users, when we reached Netscape 5.0 the version was made available as an open source program.

34

In other words, we saw the beginning of collaborative programming in the global web community and this way of thinking was by Marc, Eric, Jim and others was eons a head of its time!

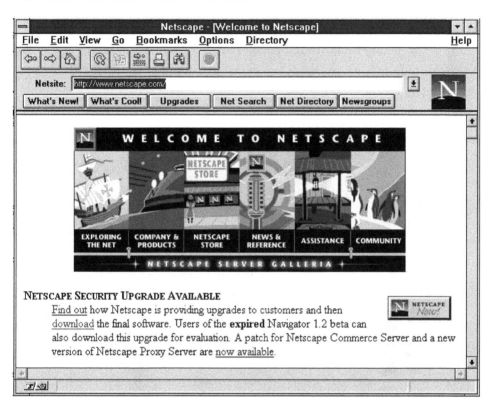

Thinking back to those early days where the Netscape 5.0 Bundle became an open source program, saw the birth of Mozilla and eventually Firefox.

So I believed the same concept had to be applied for the whole of the World Wide Web concerning web site efficiency and packet data in relation to images, media and PDF files etc. To make the World Wide Web a more efficient environment as it further evolved.

It was also from experience of the past, that I was able to remember and relate to how we downloaded huge programs and updates in the mid 90's to early 2000's in the form of zip files. Where the data files and programs were compressed, so they could be downloaded faster and easier as the data packets were far smaller in size using 7 zip and WinZip, as two popular program examples of the day!

So when confronted with the reality of the bounce rate and the knowledge of knowing as more and more packet data and users came online there will be greater delays, chaos and a forever greater challenge for the global community.

Creating The New Internet Super Highway

Compress Der World Wide Web!

**Einstein's School
of Dino Web DNA**

By Alastair Agutter

Then it suddenly dawned on me, what if we could in fact start to "flat pack" the World Wide Web!!!

At the same time, thinking of a way to create a "free" collaborative program that every web site owner could begin to use and participate in, for a new World Wide Web environment called "The New Internet Super Highway."

Such an environment was possible to create by looking and thinking at the situation not as a physical world consisting of PC's and Servers, but as a "Virtual World" consisting of data and programs.

The World Wide Web in many respects is an alien life force entity today that is constantly growing and evolving by the day as an artificial intelligence in a different dimension we know as a "Virtual World" that is Naturally Branching and forever growing as an artificial intelligence life form and in fact mirroring the dark energy in the universe we know exists. Again, a subject I wrote about in "The Theory of Particle Matter Frequencies and Multiple Universes" to help folk understand what dark energy is, in the form of particle matter data strings, nodes and foot prints!

QUOTATION

"My only fear with humanity regarding anything of beauty involving technology can so often be made ugly from greed and ignorance."

~ Alastair R Agutter

THE WORLD'S LARGEST VIRTUAL WORLD COLLABORATIVE PROJECT

As society evolves through technology, here again Natural Law is demonstrating with Quantum Mechanics, how it can remove borders and boundaries surrounding the World of Politics and Governments.

The reality of creating "The World's Largest Virtual World Collaborative Project" to deliver "The New Internet Super Highway" is no longer dependent or reliant on Governments or Policies. But citizens of the World who own personal web sites or technology entities and seek to engage in this new virtual world!

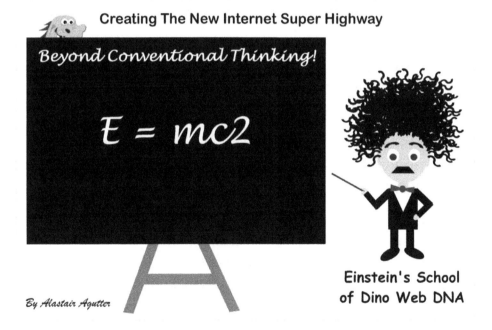

Creating The New Internet Super Highway

Beyond Conventional Thinking!

$$E = mc2$$

By Alastair Agutter

Einstein's School of Dino Web DNA

The other great and fascinating fact about all of this is that as an individual web site owner or independent entity, you can engage in this new "free" project to immediately start to change the web site or online enterprise to create greater opportunities. For it has been demonstrated above in the book and again here, that the calculation surrounding Quantum Mechanics is "Infinite" and therefore any participation will create more efficiency and the equating calculation at every stage will always be correct and a positive.

The more who participate in this Collaboration Project, the faster the new World Wide Web will become. But again, Quantum Mechanics demonstrates that if others choose not to participate in the project, this will not hinder your efforts, for if you work with Quantum Mechanics and the Collaborative Project by "Shape Shifting," your packet data in the form of a vehicle of transfer will be able to defy logic and travel faster and more efficiently, regardless of the distance or the amount of traffic!

Hot Diddly Dam, I hear you Say!

At this point, you can imagine the buzz I am getting writing this book regarding a whole new world and way of thinking. Yes, it is very exciting to say the least, and I am just glad that I am able to share this information with all citizens of World!

Now you may say that this is impossible regarding the traffic currently in existence cluttering up the World Wide Web system. But the answer again is no and this is where it gets even more interesting!

Packet Data can be transported (data signalling rates) on the World Wide Web by many means using the Internet with fibre optics, copper, wireless etc. Some systems however, perform better than others, due to interference such as electromagnetic anomalies, or regarding the type of data being carried.

Now the reality is that your web data in the form of your home page being delivered to your web user, may go through many different forms of delivery trunking systems light, copper, wireless etc.

However, how often do we ever really consider this, the truthful answer is probably never by most folk. But companies such as Cisco Systems and IBM (Big Blue) do and it does make a real massive difference to their businesses and the products they offer!

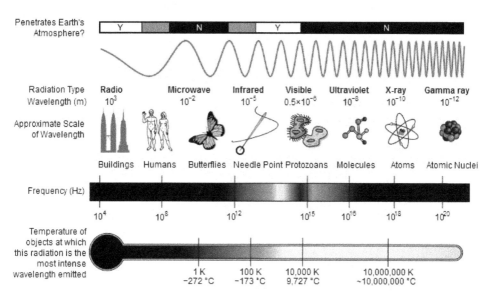

Spectrum Diagram of variant frequencies above courtesy of colleagues at Nasa.Gov

It was from studying data packet transfer by Benoit B. Mandlebrot. who became an IBM fellow, discovered the World of fractal maths in the Computer Sciences industry and found how the same size of packet data could react and perform differently through systematic tests and with varying results in relation to times and speeds.

Upon drilling down, he also realized there can be found order in the form of very simple rules, but on mass there were many variants and these could be very significant and with many facets. Be it in relation to packet data, land mass coast lines, forests regarding tree life volume and formations, to even the formation of clouds and water content. But he also realized symmetry (Natural Branching) can be found in all and the linear process of thinking and measuring by humans, is as I have referred to earlier, only a one dimensional form of thinking, both as a process and in thought.

At this point and in this discussion, here again, it is also demonstrating how Quantum Mechanics can defy the conventional rules of science as we know it in our logical way of thinking.

In the following diagram I have drawn, I can show over the same distance how you can arrive at two different outcomes, as a result you can then begin to consider the incredible impact and magnitude surrounding the subject of fractal maths. It also demonstrates why there can be inconsistencies regarding packet data transfer.

The diagram demonstrates in visual terms the variation of length over the same distance surrounding fractal maths.

Fractal Maths Diagram Example

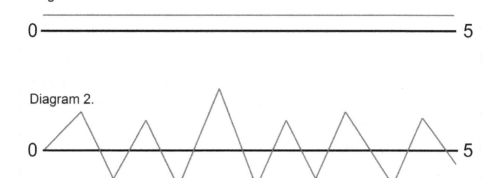

Fractal Maths Diagram by Alastair R Agutter

In diagram one, shows the top red line travelling from zero to five in a linear form. In diagram two, it shows the bottom red jagged line travelling from zero to five over the same distance, but in fractals and when measured, the second line is far longer in length.

If you translate the above examples into packet data form, it means the packet data in diagram two would be larger than the packet data in diagram one. But the time and distances can be measured as equal.

In the past five to ten years as a result of the advancements in the Sciences. Quantum Mechanics is becoming forever more understood and how it affects all our lives and how it in fact functions all around us.

As I often say and it is important to remember, in Natural Law when you examine Quantum Mechanics it is ever only seeking "positive" outcomes. For Quantum Mechanics is seeking to "evolve and refine" and in the world of the Computer Sciences today, we would term such activity as "workarounds" and this is carried out every day concerning this subject and especially seen in programming.

I have in fact myself created and actioned "workarounds" when presented with a problem and where the technical authoring architecture of a web site does not conform to complaint standards set down. The solution I devise when presented with the problem does eventually meet the compliant standards and in most instances provides a far more efficient and effective resilient solution to the problem. This is especially relevant at this time surrounding HTML 5.1 that is still in a development stage!

Above I highlighted the word "positive" in relation to outcomes for in the World of Science we believe regarding all that we know surrounding the "big bang" and particle matter, there must always be a "positive and a "negative" element to cancel each other out.

So regarding the World of Quantum Mechanics and the journey to "evolve and refine," I ask then, where are these "negative" elements to equal out.

The above again is an example of how Quantum Mechanics as a calculation is "infinite" and can be anyone or anything and therefore defies the mechanical logic and thought process of humans when we look to the stars for answers.

I have mentioned earlier in the book my close admiration and affinity I have for "Albert", Mr Einstein. Well Albert Einstein had a similar regard and affinity for a fellow Philosopher and Mathematical Physicist few people know, but is described today in the corridors of Nobel Peace Prize Winner Physicists, as "the Einstein of his day," and that man in question was James Clerk Maxwell. This genius was a Scottish Philosopher and Physicist and at a very early age, was regarded by his peers as a mathematical genius and took a post at Kings College in London, as the Professor for Maths. Now I can fully appreciate such an individual, as my elder Brother (Anthony Leonard Dobbins) of 14 years my senior, when at the same Kings College in London was also a mathematical genius and offered the post as the Professor for Maths, just before he left at a very young age in the early 1960's.

Now regarding mathematical geniuses and having one in the family, they can achieve the impossible and can calculate simultaneously multiple equations!

James Clerk Maxwell took great interest in the work of Michael Faraday some years later in his career, after making a mathematical calculation as to what the Saturn rings consisted of! Michael Faraday was working in the field of electromagnetism and electromagnetic induction, to mention just two areas.

It was in fact James Clerk Maxwell that made the Mathematical calculations surrounding the existence of electromagnetic waves. At the time of this major breakthrough, the Science community were thinking and functioning in mechanical constructive concepts based on the industrial age, so there were many sceptics regarding something that had a mathematical calculation they could not see!

Sadly James Clerk Maxwell, died at the early age of just 48 years on the 5th of November in 1879. He never saw confirmation of his discovery in his life time and it was many years later, that a German Scientist named Heinrich Rudolph Hertz, who was the first to conclusively confirm Maxwell's mathematical theory in 1886. Hertz the name we are most accustomed to surrounding radio and frequencies.

The relevance to the above here concerning our subject now as we embark on a new journey of discovery in the "Virtual World" is to appreciate again with Quantum Mechanics, all and everything is possible and not necessarily visible to the naked human eye based on the frequencies of light in the form of radiation that allows us our sight for seeing objects or other things before us.

The possibility of more frequencies is clearly demonstrated above in the diagram surrounding the electromagnetic waves spectrum, and across such a spectrum there is a greater diversity of activity that can and does exist. Eventually there will be found many sub sectors surrounding this subject and in other words, many more facets that we have yet to understand or know in the Science community in relation to human advancement and development.

So when I had my Eureka moment, with regards to "compressing" the World Wide Web and understanding the presence of Quantum Mechanics in a Virtual World. I knew I just had to establish some ground rules that could sit and exist within the World of Natural Law and Quantum Mechanics.

Natural Law teaches us in the World of Quantum Mechanics simple rules can exist and can create a positive environment of varying efficiency. A good example of this is with regards to the game of tennis.

In such a game as Tennis, a number of simple rules exist and must be adhered too. But regarding the actual playing of the game, there can be many shots, variable speeds and techniques used.

So regarding "The Creating of the New Internet Super Highway" by "Compressing" the World Wide Web in a Virtual World, I just had to devise some simple rules to achieve efficiency and success, but at the same time, a set of rules that could be retained, but allows techniques and methods to organically grow, evolve and vary!

The first rule of thumb and shared sentiments expressed by Sir Tim Berner's Lee and myself is that the World Wide Web must always be free, to ensure a greater and more informed society for human advancement.

Technology advancement as like any advances today comes with it greater responsibility as the window of error grows forever smaller, as more scientific advancements are made as mentioned earlier in the book.

So regarding today's society that functions as an international global community, any man-made advancements now will create an impact on a global community scale. Therefore, the devising of computer games for example or promoting death and conflict is an appropriate example of how technology can be used to serve to the detriment of society and is completely irresponsible and so often solely driven by money. Such a vile concept of modern day capitalism in a populated global community today is inherently flawed, and in history the evidence is there for all to see, to substantiate such a fact from the fall of the Roman Empire to the current day!

So what are the simple rules and component elements required to create a "Global Collaborative Project" with the aim to "flat packing" the World Wide Web!

The first thing we need to understand is the environment that such a project has to function in, a topic thus far we have briefly touched upon throughout the book.

For example, we know that the World Wide Web is rapidly expanding each day and with more additional packet data and computer users. We also know that States are endeavouring to try and keep up with demand by the laying of more trunking and the greater availability of 4G networks to carry such packet data.

To host such demand now and in the future, it does start with infrastructure in the form of packet data transportation networks by and between the telecommunications operators and providers of every State. As mentioned earlier, such methods and forms vary considerably and in fact, still in many parts of Britain exists no copper, but "composite" in the ground, that was used as cabling and trunking during and after World War Two, due to the shortage of copper material.

The best way I can relate to such a geographical landscape and environment for readers to follow, is to see telecom carriers as a visual and how the connectivity networks function, regarding the World Wide Web. This is to look at our telecommunication networks as if they were road systems, consisting of motorways, major "A" roads, "B" roads, lanes and pathways.

All such roads and pathways we know can and do exist, with varying obstacles of congestion and distances. As human beings regarding our thought processes and as mentioned earlier, we are more inclined to seek the quickest and most efficient route, based more on visual judgement initially from map reading and then opting in most cases for motorway routes as a president. This was certainly the case before the introduction of any computerized route map sites were devised, or found on the World Wide Web as they are today.

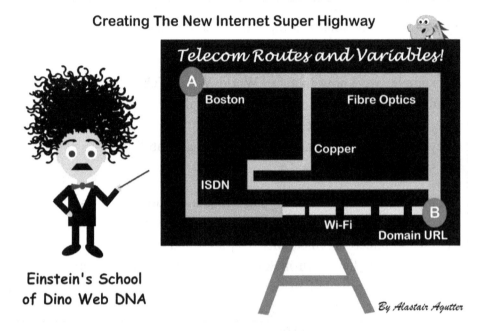

Creating The New Internet Super Highway

Telecom Routes and Variables!

A

Boston

Fibre Optics

Copper

ISDN

B

Wi-Fi

Domain URL

Einstein's School
of Dino Web DNA

By Alastair Agutter

As like any journey, there exists a starting point and a destination (A to B). So the web user of a technology device located say at Boston in the United States of America, this being the starting point (A) of their journey. When they then next enter the http (hyper-text transfer protocol) address line (web domain), this then becomes the web user's intended destination (B) say New York for example.

When the web user presses the return button on their keyboard (A) after entering their intended destination http address, a request is then sent between the web users hardware device (A) to the web server hosting the address we know as a web domain (B). This request is achieved by the connectivity of the two devices, by using IP addresses (Internet Protocol) and when contact is made, it is known as a "handshake" and a request is made for the packet data to be exchanged between the two computer devices. The packet data will consist of many elements to complete the destination (URL) web sites landing page.

This packet of data regarding the web landing page in many cases comprises of a number of different program file formats that are all made legible by the html framework structure we know as RDF (Resource Document Format). Today the Html framework has evolved further beyond Html 4.01+ to Html 5.01 today, but a structure still under development and refinement by members of the World Wide Web Consortium (WC3).

Above Picture of a Microsoft Internet Explorer Browser Program

For the web user to be able to access this environment and travel across the Virtual World of the World Wide Web, requires a program installed on their hardware device called a "Browser" Software Program bundle. The most common of these used today are; - Google Chrome, Microsoft Internet Explorer, Mozilla Foundation Fire Fox, Apple Safari and Opera to mention a good few!

To create a successful set of rules to develop a successful collaborative program to flat pack data on the World Wide Web, is to ensure all of the World's webmasters and entities can participate. This requires the full understanding of knowing who are the players, actors and the elements!

So once contact is made between a web users Laptop PC for example with the Domain Names Web Hosting Server, in the form of a hand shake and request. The packet data transfer process begins in the form of downloading the web page so it can be displayed on the web user's device by using the web browser software.

The term download can in many respects make the process sound simple and straight forward. But if you are located in Boston (A) and requesting the download packet from New York (B), this data does in fact have to travel now this distance and so if we say the distance is 1,500 miles for example. This means this data request travelling to and from back to the requesting computer is a round trip of 3,000 miles. If the web page consists of say 10 elements, this means these 10 data elements travel 1,500 miles each to the requested destination and this when totalled equals some 15,000 miles.

On the following page is another illustration where we have 10 data packet elements travelling. Now one would assume that all data will travel the same route to the requested destination, but this is not the case.

The data will not discriminate regarding distance or time and the two computers will transfer the packet data elements by the most efficient means regardless of time, distance or ease of route.

As the data is downloaded, a series of requests are made as explained between the user's Computer and the Domain Name Web Server Computer and this process depends on the number of component parts that make up the web page in the form of the number of varying program files involved.

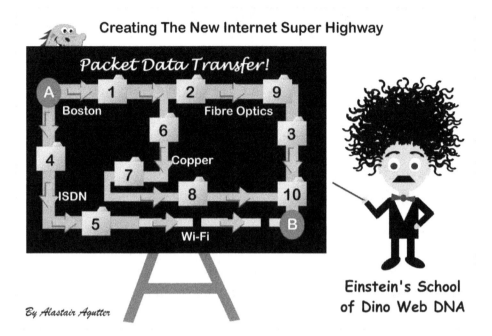

Creating The New Internet Super Highway

Einstein's School
of Dino Web DNA

The series of requests are dependent upon how many files there are in existence in relation to the web page creation, these files being the overall packet data to be transferred. These packet data files may be for example text, images, Mp3, Mp4, Gif's, Jpeg's, CSS3, HTML pages etc. All of these packet data files will vary in size and format. The latter here also relates to both browser software and computer programs, for they need to be able to understand the data being delivered and captured, before it can be displayed. A good example here is if a web page has a macromedia flash file. The only time the Browser and Computer will be able to understand such data, is when a Flash Player has been downloaded from Adobe and also the need for a plugin installation on the browser program software.

The size of a web page file as you can gather is not the only element factor in the grand scheme of things the more we understand how Natural Law works in the form of Quantum Mechanics.

As a developer or webmaster and as part of your professional activities, you will no doubt be using different types of browser software programs to test and check out your work. You may have found from such activity some browser software appears to be more proficient than others in relation to certain packet data file types. Such observations I can assure you are correct and not the case of you imagining this!

In the early processing days of Pentium and AMD in direct competition of each other, it was commonly recognized that Pentium Processors performed better with regards to gaming and multimedia programs. Whereas AMD processors performed better and were seen as more reliable when it came to business programs and word processing activities. However today, with the advancement of processor technology in the form of Quad Core and others, the days referred too are thankfully long gone.

However, such variations in processing development and technology does point out again, as a result of living in a Capitalist Society today, it shows how technology and human advancement is hindered at times, as a result of the desire for individual profit before collective effort!

I hope as the Human Race further advances to meet the challenges of today and tomorrow regarding Climate Change, causing more prevalent diseases and conflict. Capitalism as the root cause will either mature, or eventually become consigned to the history books, as the human race must finally set aside a childlike mentally and start to collectively work together in the interests of all and not for the few!

One of the biggest setbacks still today in the human advancement story of development surrounding technology and especially regarding the World

Wide Web is Capitalism (greed), to gain product advantage and as a result failing to meet universal compatibility standards.

My very youngest Child and Daughter Ellenna, recently pointed out to me her frustration with regards to the various formats of multimedia and what will work on some devices and not on others, in relation to Apple vs Microsoft, or Apple vs Samsung surrounding operating systems, namely Windows, Apple Mac and Android.

The above examples of self-interest clearly demonstrates again how the marvels of technology can also be hi-jacked and made ugly to serve the interests of some for profit and self-indulgent material wealth.

Such ideals and primitive modes of thinking goes against the whole ethos of the World Wide Web, that is in the 20th Century a wonder of the World and an environment unimaginable for greater enlightenment and founded on the values of it being made available for all. Such values and sentiments I totally and firmly endorse, in the interest of all miracles we have come to love and know, who look to us today as the primate specie of the World to do the right thing for all life on Earth.

Today in the World of technology surrounding Society, Arts and Culture and then drilling down more towards our friends who design and develop platforms online in the form of creative web sites and services. I always consider the open source community, in respect of programs and applications that can be used as free, as serving the interests of the World with reference to greater advancement and evolution of Mankind and the entity we know as the World Wide Web.

Such thoughts and ideologies I seriously considered when establishing the rules to enabling a Global Community Project that is free for flat packing the World Wide Web as I say!

THE PRIMARY ELEMENTS

To help make further ease and understanding of the number of elements or associated program files that a web site home page and other web pages comprise of in the way of packet data. I have presented the following two diagrams and images, where I have used my own home page as an example to help breakdown the actors and players that need to be identified and the ones that need to be introduced into the free collaborative project as the rules of the game as they say, with regards to flat packing the World Wide Web's web sites that host the packet data in the form of programs, applications and information.

Identifying Web Site Elements!

by Alastair Agutter

As we consider the segments that form the packet data, remember to consider this is just some of the component parts and not all of them or the whole story. As there are many more facets and factors that need to be considered, as pointed out earlier with regards to how Natural Law in the form of Quantum Mechanics and Natural Branching operates and functions.

Identifying Web Site Elements!

by Alastair Agutter

When we start to upload any information onto a Web Server for the Global Community to access and use, this means packet data that exists in some size and some form. Whilst we will respect the rules of Natural Law and apply the same rules surrounding the subject areas of Quantum Mechanics and Natural Branching, we will invariably meet anomalies that appear to be a contradiction at times in relation to our normal way of thinking. But this can be expected for regrettably society is principally based on one dimensional thinking and greatly dependent upon visual aids when it comes to understanding.

We must constantly remind ourselves that the World of Quantum Mechanics is not one dimensional and can be anything, any time or any moment and the equation at that point will always be correct. Quantum Mechanics also defies the founding beliefs surrounding positive and negative particle matter elements, for Quantum Mechanics does not believe in negative and nor does Natural Branching as the two go hand in hand to Naturally Branch and create more and Quantum Mechanics functions to provide the engineering answers and intricacies to "evolve and refine" as the journey continues with regards to all that we know and do not know at this time in our human journey of learning.

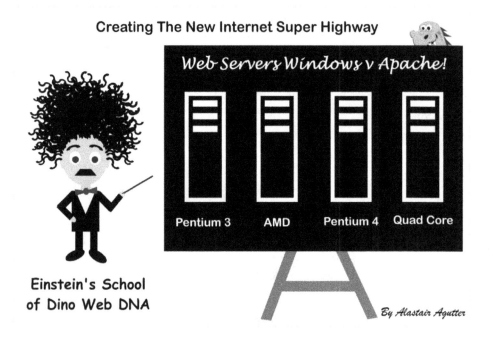

From the uploading of a single web home page we need to appreciate behind the scenes of such a presentation exists the functioning of the web server itself in relation to its age and processing ability. We also need to consider the operating system efficiency commonly in the form of Windows or Apache. Such environments have a bearing on the delivery of web site pages and any other programs or applications housed on the web server for downloading.

We also need to consider the web user accessing the information on the web server in relation to the hardware device type they are using and its capabilities. In between such hardware technology devices for exchanging data we then have to consider the connectivity in the form of telecommunications networks trunking as mentioned earlier.

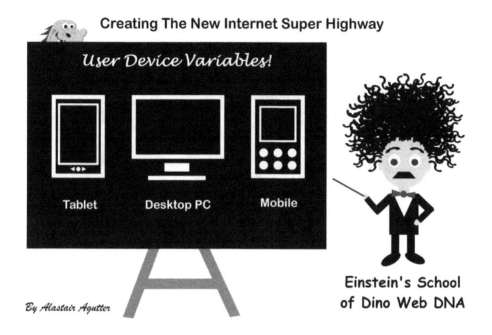

All of the above have a bearing and relevance to the successful delivery of packet data be it in the form of a web site and web pages or programs and applications to be downloaded.

As discussed earlier these environments can be varied and as pointed out so can be the case in relation to web servers and web user devices.

However what we can see and understand from the realization of the above factors, it is sensible to co-exist and work with Natural Law and especially with regards to Quantum Mechanics concerning the founding principles to "evolve and refine", thus in turn seeking "simplistic perfection" and therefore delivering a healthier packet data environment.

These values should be especially relevant and pertinent when we examine society today where chaos is abound with constant frenzied activities and where very many are not conducive to one's health.

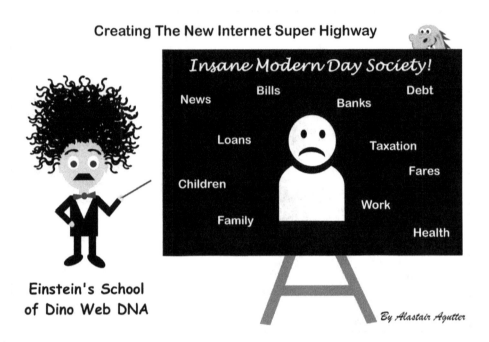

The human condition very often unknowingly seeks equilibrium, very often when relaxing quietly and without any interruption is a time where the human entity finds a passive mode of existence. The act of not doing anything in many respects is a safe place, for any action one takes will always have consequence and these can be positive or negative dependent upon purpose and interpretation.

From such moments of peace, it is a good example of understanding risk aversion and such factors in any environment are essential.

From the very beginning of the human story risk aversion has played a very important role in the lives of human beings and in many ways. The realization surrounding the consequences in conflict is a good example or the avoidance of large cat species when hunting for food on the African plains.

As you can see from greater discussion in this chapter there are many factors and facets in play even when we consider the delivery of just a web site between the web user and web server hosting the data.

One of our greatest failings today in human evolution is from technology, where many are becoming reliant on the functionality of technology to eliminate environment activities, rather than shaping technology to work with the human condition to gain greater enlightenment. As a result, human society in most respects, is becoming more superficial with regards to today's technology serving as an aid and yet still having a subconscious desire for continued or greater activity by the human being condition.

Our greatest scientist in the 20th Century Albert Einstein alluded to such concerns for the future when he quoted, "I fear the day that technology will surpass our human interaction. The world will have a generation of idiots." ~ Albert Einstein.

The World Wide Web today as discussed earlier in this book, most succinctly demonstrates how there is an ever increasing greater demand for using technology and none more so than with the emergence of Social Media that aptly demonstrates greater human activity, the bulk of which being of a superficial nature!

Such environments and technology advances in the form of Social Media, where technology device hardware works in conjunction with such platforms and form a key essential part of a human beings activity in society, is not necessarily good for a human being's personal health or advancement, namely education and enlightenment.

The key points raised in the above paragraphs, demonstrates admirably again, how such an environment that is to serve humanity and all life for the greater good and the preservation of the planet, is not necessarily a clear cut straight forward case or just one dimensional.

So to be part of a new Virtual World in the form of "The New Internet Super Highway" and at the same time continue an existence in relation to the status quo environment in the form of the existing Internet or World Wide Web. Like Scientists and Engineers in pursuit of seeking to achieve space travel at the rate of the speed of light, we have to advance the design of our vehicle or virtual world space station, once we have established the element factors that require attention and alteration.

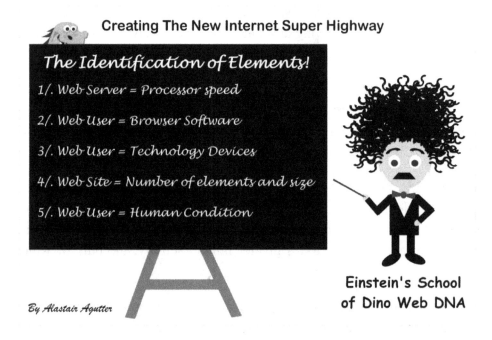

Creating The New Internet Super Highway

The Identification of Elements!

1/. Web Server = Processor speed

2/. Web User = Browser Software

3/. Web User = Technology Devices

4/. Web Site = Number of elements and size

5/. Web User = Human Condition

By Alastair Agutter

Einstein's School of Dino Web DNA

As I often refer to the DNA of Particle Matter where there are many sub atomic particles and many more to be discovered. Here in identifying the elements surrounding the World Wide Web and the new internet super highway, we have to first consider primary categories and then sub categories involved and present as we drill down more, surrounding the subject.

So let us first consider and take the identified primary categories and then expand from here.

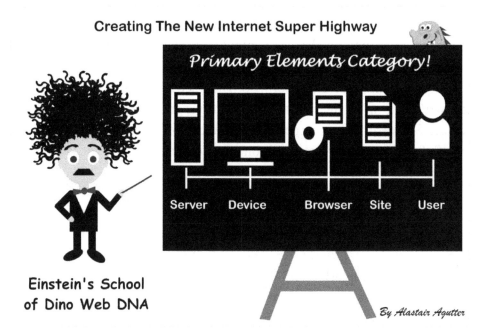

1/. The Web Server

This entity element is the storage facility for retaining our packet data in the form of web sites and programs and then made available upon user requests via various browser programs and device types.

2/. Technology Device

Today as we know technology devices come in many forms from Tablet, Desktop PC, Smart Phones, Laptops, Notebooks, Netbooks and Smart TV. They operate as the end users device vehicle to gain access to the Internet and World Wide Web by connecting to the respective host web server storing the packet data by using IP address connectivity.

3/. Browser Software

Browser software is the program that allows the end users device to be able to interpret and display the content from the World Wide Web in the form of web pages and also the ability to download additional programs and plugins. There are many forms of Browser Software Programs created and written to meet the operating system programming on the end users device. Some of the most popular Browser software bundles being Fire Fox, Safari, Internet Explorer, Chrome and Opera etc.

4/. Web Site

The web site is a program created and written in the RDF (Resource Definition Framework) HTML environment. Web site creation encompasses many different programs that can be bolted onto the HTML environment. Today Html 5.01 (RDFa) is the most recent standard of architecture for web development and browser readability. Many web sites today at the time of publishing this book still use Html 4.01 as a standard, but now many features of this version 4.01 are becoming outdated and obsolete. Regarding the new Html 5.01 benchmark standard, this is still further undergoing development and as rule of thumb, regarding any program in development the later odd number in a program bundle means it is in a beta stage of development. Even numbers at the end of any software program indicates the program has reached a stage of completion. However, further newer versions can often become into being at a later date.

The numeric end number sequence method is a recognized standard across the whole of the programming industry.

5/. Web User

The web user is of course ourselves seeking access using the Internet to access the World Wide Web for information, products and services. As the user we are dependent on the efficiency of many technologies this starting with connectivity of our broadband or WiFi telecom providers service. The functionality and processing speed of our device and then the World Wide Web environment regarding the access of particular web sites and their speed and efficiency is based on the way they have been technically authored.

When we look at the five primary elements summarized above we can quickly conclude, if we apply a thought process of risk aversion and efficiency, there exists many factors to determine the end result being the delivery of packet data information to us fast and efficiently.

The end user is dependent upon all these technologies working at their most efficient, to hopefully deliver packet data by the most efficient means.

Here we are just covering the primary element variables and within each of these there are a whole host of other sub category elements that need to be considered.

From the human condition to all life forms, products, technology etc. the key is to seek risk aversion and this is demonstrated constantly when we understand the functions of Natural Law in universe(s) in relation to Quantum Mechanics and where it is frequently seen surrounding this subject, the signature code is to "Evolve and Refine" and so this such environment of technology we are discussing and interested in is reliant upon many other factors and elements within the "technology" subject areas. This field area requires proficiency and the elimination of elements that can expose these processes to risk and failure in many forms.

So when we consider the many variable elements even just in the primary sense itemized above, the cake factor scenario again comes into play and to the fore, where we have to consider the entire cake as the potential user audience base and then we have to try to determine and establish how we can retain such an audience level for any web site, program or platform service we seek to provide by delivering regular efficiency.

THE PRIMARY ELEMENTS SUB CATEGORIES

Here we now look at each of the primary elements sub categories, as we further understand the actors and players, exploring beyond the surface.

THE WEB SERVER ELEMENTS

Here we now look at the sub category factors of the Web Server Elements that are all relevant parts.

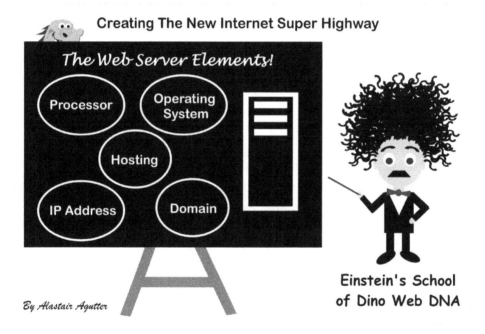

The web server device relies on many players and actors regarding its successful functionality and performance. Starting with the age of the hardware device and what I describe as under the hood to deliver speed for a demanding user environment.

Above in Albert's illustration are a number of these sub-category elements that exist within the web server device that are important for the delivery of packet data to the end user.

1/. Processor

The processing speed may seem a common sense consideration, but many web servers today still function and serve the community with varying technology abilities based on the age of the machines.

It is common place that many web servers today still run on Pentium 4 processors and still retain standard form motherboards. This can cause significant problems if you have a high volume customer demanding commercial web site selling products, when using an ecommerce programming bundle or operating a gaming platform.

2/. Operating System

Operating systems for web servers can also vary considerably, the two most common being Linux and Windows. In addition to the operating systems, are the software programs such as Apache that run and drive these web server services? Such technology programs are today becoming forever more advanced and complex, especially when we consider more security features being developed surrounding SSL (secure socket layers).

3/. Web Hosting

Web hosting can come in many forms and package sizes, offered by the Web Server Hosting Provider for storing a webmasters web site. Dedicated Web Server Hosting is popular with more demanding webmaster services in the way of ecommerce and gaming. More educational and informed service web sites can share services, as they are normally far smaller in size and traffic levels are often lower due to specialist subject areas covered.

4/. IP Address

IP Address is the assigned internet protocol number of the Web Server, so computer devices and web servers can connect with each other. Webmasters who share web server storage space with others can in most cases acquire and buy a dedicated IP Address from the web server hosting provider. This gives a unique number in relation to the webmasters web site in question.

5/. Domain Name

Domain Names are the web site's identification and this name is then programmed to marry up with the related IP Address that corresponds to the web site's web server hosting the service.

On a Web Server there are also many other required server program features that include Mail Servers, Black and White Server Lists, Sub Domain configuration and Programming, Anti-Spam and Virus Programs. Most if not all of these programs and service features are relevant and important to the function of the service provided by the web site venue.

Therefore it is important to remember technical authoring and programming of the web site or the web server of any kind for these services to function efficiently and properly, requires the highest of standards for every error comes delay and performance problems.

Within the Web Server and Web Hosting environment you can see as we discuss this first primary category element the many sub category element factors that can give rise to function, efficiency and performance problems.

It also demonstrates how important connectivity is between many elements to deliver packet data successfully from point A) being the Web Server to point B) being the User's device. Now if we think beyond the realms of one dimensional thinking with regards to the human condition, such anomalies to consider can also in many respects be a positive, as it also demonstrates the many facets that can be explored regarding the Laws of Quantum Mechanics surrounding the subject of refinement.

So then we reach another pivotal point and subject area in our understanding, as we reach beyond the shackles of one-dimensional thinking and come to terms with the realms of "Human Enlightenment" and where from every negative we can also find and discover a positive.

Just recently Morgan Freeman the great American actor was featured in a documentary programme for television examining religions, faiths and apocalypse beliefs. In the programme he was fortunate to visit a Tibetan Monk, where he gained from the meeting a greater understanding of enlightenment.

Enlightenment helps to begin an understanding of ones journey in relation to all that we see and cannot see. Attached to this growing understanding is that all exists in cycles and within such cycles there is a beginning and an end. In between two such events is a journey of discovery and learning where can be found simplistic perfection, beauty and refinement leaving any wise individual humbled.

QUOTATION:

"Enlightenment is a growing understanding when on ones journey of learning, that all exists in cycles. With a start, humble end and a new beginning."

~ Alastair Agutter

TECHNOLOGY DEVICE ELEMENTS

Here we now look at the sub category factors of the Technology User Device Elements that are all relevant parts.

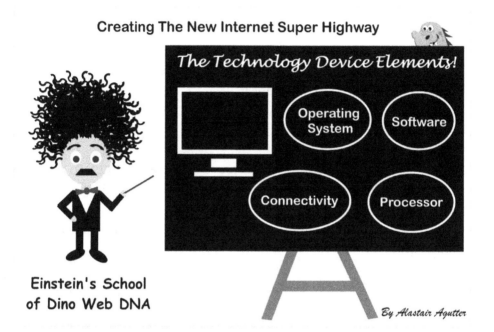

1/. Operating System

Today we know there are many user device types that now access the World Wide Web via the Internet and many of these user technology hardware devices are in the form of Desktop PC's, Tablets, Mobile Smart Phones and Laptops etc. and using many varying different operating systems such as Microsoft Windows, Linux, Macintosh (Mac) and Android.

The user device operating system's performance is based upon the actual authoring of such robust software technology and the user hardware device's capabilities in relation to processing ability speeds and device age.

Referring back to the "Cake" scenario it needs to be any developer or programmers intention to reach the entire cake when we relate this to the world-wide geographical audience base and their new and used respective devices.

All operating systems have varying design features to meet global community user demands as business users, consumer to academia. Such operating systems can therefore perform well, better or fair dependent upon the fields and disciplines being undertaken or covered.

Today, Internet configuration and access is very much a built in norm for most recent operating system developments. However, again age of a device and certain parts of more outpost regions of the world do often experience problems through connectivity and this also needs to be considered.

2/. Software

Software again in relation to performance is based upon the capabilities of the device in relation to age and processing ability to allow an operating system to function effectively and efficiently. Other important considerations in relation to an operating system and software performance when using the Internet and accessing the World Wide Web relates to processor hardware, graphics and multimedia cards technology ability, and if they are up to speed and of a standard for the operating system and software programs to successfully function, especially in relation to connectivity and browser software.

3/. Connectivity

Varying forms of connectivity is possible today across many different user device types. However connectivity speeds and performance are based upon carrier trunking methods, regions, locations and the actual mode of connectivity in the form of modem copper, broadband, ISDN and Wi-Fi etc. Again connectivity is a key sub category element in relation to the user device when using the Internet and accessing the World Wide Web.

4/. Processor

The user device processing speed is critical when it comes to the successful access of the World Wide Web via the Internet and especially in relation to being able to view in a quick and efficient manner many forms and types of web sites. Some of these web sites and services include entertainment and ecommerce that can have a considerable burden on any hardware device's processor.

The above again shows that these sub category elements surrounding the user's device also have a significant bearing when it comes to the ease of accessing the World Wide Web via the Internet successfully. Such performance aspects can be improved and changed in such a scenario so the user experience is greatly improved.

THE BROWSER SOFTWARE ELEMENTS

Here we now look at the sub category factors of the Browser Software Elements that are all relevant parts.

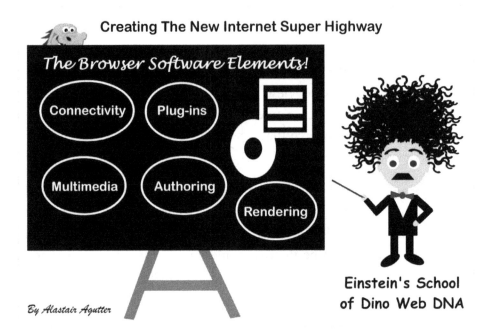

Creating The New Internet Super Highway

The Browser Software Elements!

Connectivity · Plug-ins · Multimedia · Authoring · Rendering

Einstein's School of Dino Web DNA

By Alastair Agutter

1/. Connectivity

Browser software as a sub category element is dependent upon good connectivity and the processing abilities of the user device. Connectivity as mentioned comes in many different forms and variables of speed and efficiency. Such connectivity configurations often include the use of routers and switches. These Networking environments often constitute home or business networks where a number of users can access the same connectivity provider service. DCHP as a frequent norm in respect of connectivity can hinder to a degree performance. Designated configurations on the other hand of local area networks using assigned IP addresses and sub masks (255.255.255.0) can help improve speed and performance for the browser software and thus in turn the user.

2/. Plug-ins

Plug-ins as a sub category element admirably demonstrates the very many facets as we explore further the players and actors surrounding the successful delivery of packet data. With the diversity of web design today, comes the need for plug-ins, often known as bolt on applications, to aid and assist browser software in reading, interpreting and delivering the relevant medium in question. Common examples relate to Rich Media content in the form of Shockwave Flash Media, Audio Mp3 and Video Mp4 to mention just some.

Surrounding this sub-category element and others to follow we see also the complexities and conundrums surrounding cross platform compatibility. This subject area is a serious issue that needs to be heavily thought out and considered when developing and deploying web site venues and services for the visiting user of many devices and regions from around the World.

3/. Multimedia

Browser Software rendering regarding the sub category element of Multimedia has always presented many problems and continues to do so today for very many developers and programmers. From Browser Software Programmers, Webmaster Developers to the end user, compatibility across this medium has been one of great frustration where there has been a continued variation and difference in Rich Media Formats. As a result some Android Tablet users for example, they are unable to play certain other operating system Rich Media and the same case can be for users of Apple Smart Phones surrounding other similar Rich Media Programs and Formats.

Such a landscape is one of commercial interest placed before the global community interests and therefore a webmaster developer must consider these scenarios and set in place contingencies to ensure the visiting user experience is enjoyable and complete.

4/. Authoring

Browser Software is reliant on good technical Authoring when expected to read and interpret a software presentation from any web site. Poor technical authoring of any web site causes massive delays as requests for packet data is constantly repeated many times over, to try and understand the coding in question.

Again such a sub-category element throws up the importance and significance in the grand scheme of things when we relate to speed and efficiency.

5/. Rendering

Rendering of packet data is part of another significant Sub-Category element and one briefly covered in the previous section surrounding technical authoring.

Every Browser Software has a rendering engine to deliver, read and interpret the content for web user viewing in an html format presentation.

When technically authored poorly delays can be significant and very often from constant requests to the web server for more literate coding and can often result in a 404 message and timing out from the web server that the browser software is trying to access and endeavouring to interpret the packet data in question.

Sadly surrounding this subject sub category element topic many web developers and programmers of web site coding fail to appreciate the great importance of being Browser Software friendly and where from poor technical authoring a web sites rankings can become marked down in the web rankings on search engines where both Browser Software and Search Engine Data Mining Engines interact exchanging Meta Data intelligence.

THE WEB SITE ELEMENTS

Here we now look at some of the sub category sections surrounding the Web Site Elements that are all relevant parts.

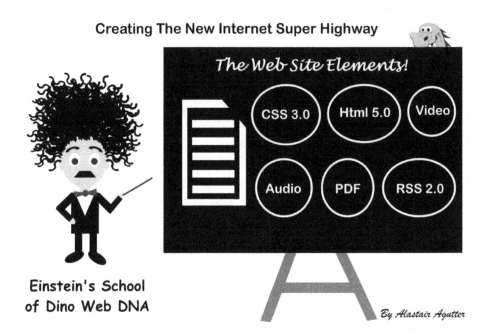

1/. Html 5.0

Html is the main core shell for all web sites. Other programs and coding is simply bolt on to the HTML Resource Definition Framework (RDF or RDFa). Key data is also embedded into the web site pages to assist search and browser rendering engines we know as Meta Data or Meta Tags. Html 4.01 (RDF) has been the main stay framework for many years, but now Html 5.0 (RDFa) has now eclipsed this previous coding standard.

2/. CSS 3.0

CSS (Cascading Style Sheets) as a sub category regarding web site elements is a major part of web site design today and helps take some of the heavy load of coding with the creation and development of Cascading Style Sheets (CSS). Images and design layouts can be determined by using CSS and the new standard today being CSS 3.0.

3/. Video

Rich Media content in the form of the sub category element of Video has always posed a significant frustration to webmasters and program developers as a result of commercial interests resulting in varying different formats. Therefore contingencies have to be put in place to ensure the web user experience is complete.

4/. Audio

Rich Media as a sub category element in the form of Audio is also another frustration deriving from commercial interests and where there are varying formats. Cross platform delivery here is not always possible based on the users browser and operating system and so again contingencies have to be put in place to meet the users rightful demands of viewing successfully such content created and developed.

5/. PDF

With the more recent emergence of hardware devices in the form of Ebook Readers Portable Document Framework (PDF) has seen a considerable rise in use. Also in relation to commercial operations where more up market and quality brand organizations are producing more online PDF catalogues for the web user customer to view.

6/. RSS 2.0

RSS as a sub category element I have included in some of these element examples for as a news delivery system, RSS does have great power and very often can be delivered and streamed directly to the web users Browser Software when web users sign up to Really Simple Syndication (RSS) and a good Browser example being Fire Fox.

THE WEB USER ELEMENTS

Here we now look at the sub category factors of the Web User Elements that are all relevant parts and probably the most important, as every web site wants visitors and so the environment has to be correct for this to happen.

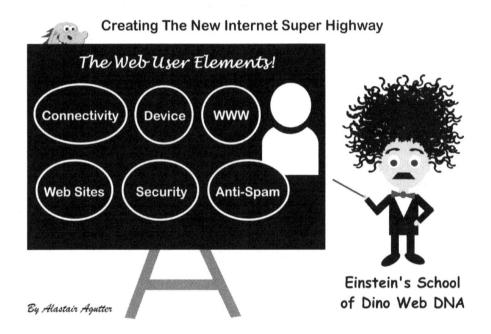

1/. Connectivity

We all know for the web user this sub category element is critical for all to happen. Connectivity is far easier to configure today, as opposed to years gone by. Most procedures relating to setting up this connectivity process today is achieved by using a step by step wizard program procedure. When on a network these procedures may become more difficult where IP Addresses are assigned and also certain designated ports are used for access, plus with many routers today they are password based for security reasons.

2/. Device

The user device as another sub category element is naturally very important and the specification of such a user device has a bearing on delivery and speed of any web site or software download in the form of Packet Data. Connectivity forms will also no doubt have a bearing in relation to the many varying differences be it Wi-Fi, Copper, Broadband and Fibre Optics etc. Regions around the World will also have a bearing and so any user device beyond the capabilities of the hardware itself, have other considerations that need to be "Evolved and Refined" by adopting and joining "The Internet Super Highway" Virtual World system.

3/. World Wide Web

This sub category element surrounds the main purpose being to access the World Wide Web invented by Sir Tim Berners-Lee of England. Both connectivity and hardware are major parts in this process for success to reach the many millions of web sites that exist today. Efficiency and successful delivery of these web sites derive from a whole stream of elements we are covering. Packet Data delivery is dependent upon the functionality of user devices, operating systems and software.

4/. Web Sites

This sub category element refers to Web Sites for acquiring information, products and services. All such web site venues consist of many elements as mentioned and all need to function with the greatest efficiency. Correct technical authoring is a key essential to the successful access of every web site world-wide and refinement is critical to reach every user and device type.

5/. Security

This sub category element is sadly a necessary requisite in today's society to protect user devices and personal data. It is a further example demonstrating the need for such continued advancements so we can rise beyond the basic forms of human behaviour that is destructive and divisive and greatly serves to the detriment of the human evolutionary story. Security in web site development and web server hosting again needs to refine and evolve to eradicate the vulnerabilities very often created from poor technical authoring.

6/. Anti-Spam

This sub category element Anti-Spam is another unfortunate evil deriving from human behaviour and so very often a trait driven for commercial reasons and without understanding the protocols and ethics that do exist in the web community and invisibly governed by the main players. The failing to adhere to the standards will result in a lack of opportunity leading to eventual online demise for any web site owner, especially in relation to black server listings. However individuals can also be black listed if they post and send unsolicited email content to the wider community with a legal risk of prosecution surrounding theft in the form of non-consent usage of user data usage under contract agreement by their telecom provider where the user has to pay for it.

As you can see from above, beyond the Primary Category elements there are very many more sub category sectors. Therefore it is very important from the very outset that our objective should be to look beyond a one-dimensional approach and form of thinking, to meet the needs of the user today regardless of location, connectivity and device capabilities to which we can address. By embracing this new way of development and thinking, regarding "The New Internet Super Highway" that now follows with the introduction of the "Ramesses Horizon Program" that I created to provide the answers and to help identify how we can adopt Sir Isaac Newton's Natural Law, in the form of Quantum Mechanics, to "Evolve and Refine" all possible elements that will serve for the greater good of all.

QUOTATION:

"Great Technology creation is when you can see beyond the horizon and understand the impact it has on humanity and all life."

~ Alastair Agutter

THE RAMESSES HORIZON

PROGRAM

The first thing to remember when you develop something in a virtual world, it can be created in many dimensional forms and therefore even invisible as a physical presence form that is functioning within an ever greater learning environment phenomena.

In this program I have identified what can be "flat packed" as I call it and therefore taking the World Wide Web to another dimension for webmasters and developers to join "The New Internet Super Highway" where their web sites will become at least 3 to 4 times faster, in other words, 300 to 400% more efficient than they currently are for a faster more seamless and enjoyable web user experience with the end result being more web user visitors (customers) and greater success online.

I am sure you will also be able to further improve performance of your web site by more than 3 to 4 times (300-400%), as you discover and examine what changes and improvements can be made.

I hope you will also find this exercise an enlightening period and moment in your creative design and development life where from technically authoring your web site correctly and changing other relevant elements, a whole new world and way of thinking will open up for you.

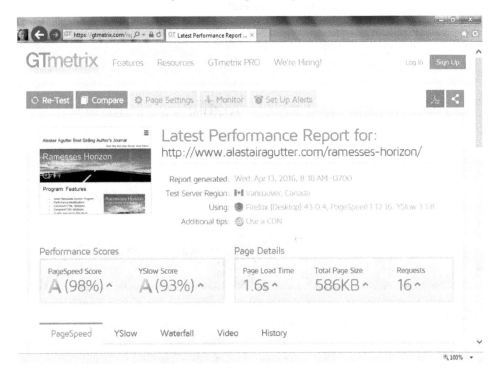

Ramesses Horizon Program

Web Site Address: www.alastairagutter.com/ramesses-horizon/

Let's now see how by joining "The New Internet Super Highway" in a Virtual World and embracing Sir Isaac Newton's Natural Law and following the rules of Quantum Mechanics, establish what we can change, evolve and refine as a new collaborative member of this new and very exclusive club at this time.

PERFORMANCE MODIFICATIONS

With regards to performance modifications we need to establish the areas we can evolve and refine. This process of establishing what can be changed took me several months, for the more I dissected I found many more elements in the equation that we have outlined and discussed as Primary Elements and Sub Category Elements.

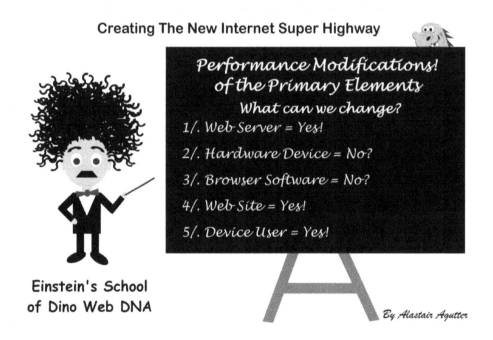

Creating The New Internet Super Highway

Performance Modifications!
of the Primary Elements
What can we change?
1/. Web Server = Yes!
2/. Hardware Device = No?
3/. Browser Software = No?
4/. Web Site = Yes!
5/. Device User = Yes!

Einstein's School of Dino Web DNA

By Alastair Agutter

1st we looked at the Primary Element sectors and these were: 1/. Web Server, 2/. Device, 3/. Browser and 4/. Web Site, 5/. The Web User.

1/. The Web Server I found can be altered and improved for performance to help connectivity and processing to deliver Packet Data requested.

2/. The User device as we know can alter considerably in specification, age and performance based on technology advancements of the day. We also know the device used can come in many forms (Desktop PC, Laptop, Notebook, Netbook, Mobile Phone, Tablet and Smart TV) so here there is little that can be done other than helping the oldest and most basic device to be able to access Packet Data via connectivity location and regions.

3/. The Browser Software is where we can assist with correctly technically authored web sites and where the Packet Data requested can be interpreted and read by the rendering engine with ease and therefore this greatly speeds up the process of delivery to the viewing web user's device.

4/. The Web Site which is the main reason for the user accessing the World Wide Web via the Internet can be greatly altered and improved for the viewing web user and these details of "How to" will follow shortly in this book.

5/. The Web User as a Primary Element for change may seem to many webmasters and program developers to be a strange consideration. But as I said at the very beginning of this book and throughout, it is now time to stop thinking one dimensionally. We can change the Web User's habits and make the access of packet data far easier, faster and more efficient believe it or not, and also take into consideration every age of user and their computing skills proficiency that is very rarely considered in truth.

WEB SERVER PERFORMANCE MODIFICATIONS

Here follows the alterations that can be made regarding Web Server performance modifications as part of "The New Internet Super Highway" Virtual World Technology advancements in a different dimension and way of thinking.

1/. Enable Gzip Compression

Gzip compression is reducing the size of your files to increase the speed of the packet data transfer to the web user's browser software. The request by the user's device to the related web server hosting the files for the packet data will invariably take longer if these packet files are larger and as a result taking longer for the content to be display on the browser software.

Gzip compression is what it is and therefore compressing the web pages on the web server before delivering the packet data files to the device user browser software and therefore dramatically reducing the delivery time.

Gzip compression is very easy to deploy and as Html and CSS is used many times with repeated coding, this data can be compressed to as much as 60 to 75% in most instances.

Browser software today is in fact programmed to determine if Gzip Compression is in force and once determined the browser software then requests the packet data in much smaller form, this being in this instance web pages.

There are many ways to add Gzip compression depending on if you have IIS or Apache server frameworks on the web server.

For Microsoft (IIS) Gzip Compression visit the following link:

https://technet.microsoft.com/en-us/library/cc771003%28v=ws.10%29.aspx

For Apache Server Gzip Compression visit the following link:

http://httpd.apache.org/docs/current/mod/mod_deflate.html

If you are not comfortable surrounding this field of expertise, please consult with a colleague who is conversant and familiar with this procedure to prevent the loss of any data.

2/. Leverage Browser Caching

With Leverage Browser Caching it is possible to place snippets of data onto the web device user's browser software to speed up the delivery time and process of displaying the web site and web pages regarding revisiting web visitors.

As we know every time a request is made for a web site or web page by the device user's browser software, this packet data has to be downloaded to display the web site pages. The files in question downloaded vary considerably in format form, some of these being Html, CSS, JavaScript and Images for example. The actual size of files can also vary considerably from a few kilobytes to several megabytes.

As a viewing web user waiting for these files to download can be a very frustrating time and the objective of this book is the elimination of such events and so every element of refinement helps to further evolve, refine and advance the process.

Each file makes an individual request as mentioned in the book earlier and so this process can take time. Browser caching helps by storing some of these files locally on a user's device and so when they re-visit the site again, a great deal of the packet data has already been downloaded and this is mainly in relation to what we describe as "the skin" which is the overall design style of the web site in relation to reoccurring buttons, icons and logo's etc.

To enable browser caching you need to edit your HTTP headers and set up expiry dates. However, this process requires a great deal of skill and if you are not familiar with the process of HTTP header editing please consult a friend or colleague who does have the respective skills and expertise.

I apologise for the latter comments above and may well repeat them several times through the book in this chapter. But I do have to point these issues out for legal reasons in the event of a procedure not being carried out correctly.

There are instances sometimes when leverage caching may not necessarily be advisable. This is if you have a new business and web site and where such a new venture has not yet become established or is known in the web community. As a result in some instances a device user's anti-spam or anti-virus software may care to block the coding string being requested to be placed on the user's device as a possible virus threat.

The above can happen and can be a frequent occurrence when using CGI (common gateway interface) on a web site design and where a message may appear, stating that this web page seeks to open an unknown program etc. In such circumstances an option message appears, asking if the user cares to block or give access. And so in these instances this can cause further delay rather than reducing the time.

3/. Avoid Landing Page Redirects

Redirects on landing pages causes massive delays for the web user accessing the service and often coined to be a round trip and here is why?

If a web site or service is linked to a certain page or location and then needs to be redirected to another page, this can run into many seconds as the packet data requests are also sent on a round trip and have to come through the same landing page redirects. So for example if a web page on average takes 2 minutes to download and is then on a redirect taking a further 30 seconds, already another additional one fifth of time delay has occurred and this is before we consider the many packet data requests to and from the hosting web server and again having to go via the landing page redirect.

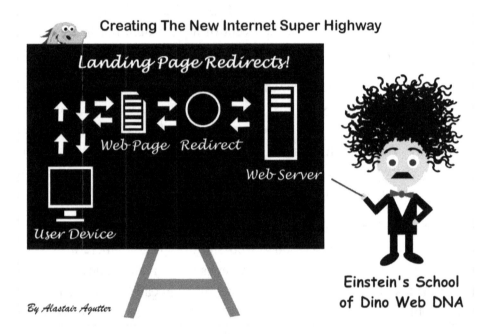

Creating The New Internet Super Highway

Landing Page Redirects!

Web Page   Redirect

Web Server

User Device

By Alastair Agutter

Einstein's School
of Dino Web DNA

If you are presented with a situation where a redirect is required due to a different location of a web server say in another Country, it is easier to make changes within the web server in question.

Redirects at any time or of any form are not friends when it comes to browser software or search engines when data mining. Try and avoid redirects at all times, as these will affect your rankings with search engines and browser software.

4/. Enable Keep Alive

Enabling HTTP keep-alive or HTTP keep connections open and persistent on a web server allows 24/7 connectivity for all forms of packet data requests. If a web server configuration is not live 24/7 when any request does come in for packet data this will cause greater delay and in many cases timing out. Keeping alive HTTP avoids such scenarios or delays in packet data transfer.

5/. Specify a Cache Validator

Any form of packet data transfer is time consuming and so by specifying expiry dates for example on a web page in the form of last updated and modified can help data mining search engines and user browser rendering engines to determine if they need to request a completely new web page for example as opposed to the existing web page in the user device temporary files of cache data stored as a revisiting web user.

Cache instructions and data can come in many forms; one of the most popular is an ETag. Instruction can be given of an expiry date or whether to request new packet data.

Now within this rule of refinement I am not necessarily convinced such tweaking in this area is for all, or even worthwhile as devices become faster and from the advancements of Html 5.0 (RDFa) with regards to complaint standard areas of improvement and refinement that is currently an ongoing operation and so we have to be very careful that such technical authoring changes will still meet compliant standards. For I can confirm regardless of what people read from the World Wide Web in relation to some tech coding sites and tutorials, a great deal of the data and coding is in fact outdated or simply flawed (not correct).

If you have a very small web site that requires regular updates across a few web pages these slight modifications maybe worthwhile. But based upon experience and taking one example such as articles written, these may never change or alter ever again.

6/. Specify a Vary: Accept Encoding Header

When you consider using varying HTTP encoding it can lead to greater risk of failure or problems and especially across public proxies that either do not allow such compressed data or simply cannot understand it. Risk aversion has been covered earlier in the book along with the rules of Quantum Mechanics which is to "evolve and refine" therefore eliminating probable's of conflict or failure is a key consideration from the very outset.

It is possible to migrate and deploy coding to permit two options of delivery, but I believe whilst such practices try to eliminate one problem of efficiency it in turn creates another.

Very often we here of the need for balance in our lives and the importance of understanding the need to reduce extreme variables across an identified spectrum field that we call risk aversion. We have also discussed the evolutionary progress and balance in Natural Law and so when presented with one option that may assist one area of advancement it may in fact serve to the detriment regarding another element.

7/. Hosting Optimization

Since the very early days of the commercial World Wide Web back in the mid 90's the costs to web hosting has come down in price considerably and continues to come down in price today.

In early times surrounding this subject many colleagues including myself use to operate our own dedicated servers for the World Wide Web Community. But as technology advanced such systems became slow and outdated.

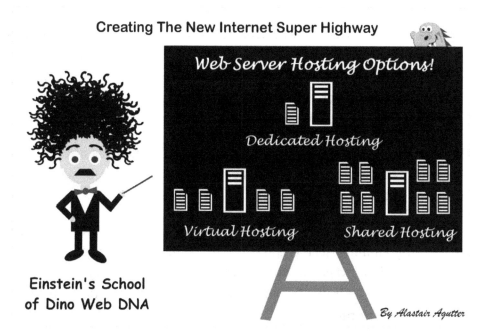

Einstein's School of Dino Web DNA

The emergence of Domain and Web Hosting providers today as new business models have become very large and prominent where considerable investment has been made around the World by these growing entities.

Today Domain Name registration services and Web Hosting providers are massively large and well established offering a plethora of different packages from around the World.

In an ideal scenario for any web site would be to have your own dedicated web server available. However, this can still be rather costly today as opposed to virtual web hosting or shared web hosting, where a web server hosts a number of web sites on one web server system device.

If restricted by a financial budget for example being an academic web site or non-profit organization and where you would have to plum for a shared web hosting package, it would be worthwhile purchasing a dedicated IP Address. For when you are sharing a web site on a web server with others you have no knowledge of knowing the credibility of the other web sites being hosted. Very often the IP Address across these web sites is the same when on a shared web server and where only two IP Addresses are normally assigned for connectivity.

The second IP Address is normally known as a fall back, as a reserve for web users seeking to access packet data from the web server and respective web site in question.

When a Web Server needs to be configured programmers and developers enter a programming sector known as a "Name Server Administration" section and this is where IP Addresses are entered to marry up with the domain name of the web site, email and other services that the web server is required to perform.

By purchasing dedicated IP Addresses you are creating a set of unique IP Addresses that are known and relate to your web site and domain name. So if there is any other skulduggery on any of the other web sites sharing the same web server, such events it will not reflect or be associated to you and your web site.

I often see advertisers and opportunists writing in to Google Adsense asking why their sites are no longer working properly, or having technical problems, or their advertising and web pages are being blocked across the web, or worse still accounts closed, so here follows the reasons why.

This is extremely important for all webmasters and developers to know. Behind the scenes and this is not common public knowledge, but there does exist an ethical standards and trust algorithm system among the really big players such as Google, Microsoft, IBM, Symantec, Oracle etc. I have in fact a ranking in this integrity measurement of "Trust" and so even individuals who have significant influence regarding technology and the World Wide Web are not immune or excluded.

So if you bend the rules should I say on one web site and your name is associated with it, any future web sites with your name will be marked down as bad or distrustful and this will stay with you for life.

There is also in existence as mentioned earlier in the book Black and White Server lists and so if you send out countless unsolicited email's to the web community as a foolish marketing plan, you will eventually become doomed to failure, as your details including your domain name will become entered onto these black server lists internationally.

Dedicated Hosting: Is where you supply and manage your own web server in a facility and hosting only your web site.

Virtual Hosting: Is where you use one of the service provider's web servers for hosting your web site.

Shared Hosting: Is what it is and where you share your web site on a web server with a number of other web sites.

USER DEVICE PERFORMANCE MODIFICATIONS

Here follows the alterations we can make to help the User's Device regarding performance as part of "The New Internet Super Highway" Virtual World Technology advancements in a different dimension and way of thinking.

1/. Enable Cross Platform Compatibility

As mentioned earlier in the book it is important to put your mind as a webmaster and program developer into the mind of the web user accessing your web site and consider the device types, age and processing ability.

The biggest mistake over countless years is where a webmaster or developer in most instances has the fastest and latest technology device hardware themselves and then proceeds to create, design and build based on the abilities and performance of these devices super doper web sites all singing and all dancing. However, what a webmaster and developer should be considering is the most basic device or system seeking to access your web site online not the most advanced.

Then again as mentioned earlier in the book you have to consider the connectivity available to the user seeking to access your web site and the device type itself.

When developing any web site it must be cross platform complaint, otherwise the potential audience base will be considerably reduced and in large numbers taking us back to the big cake scenario based on the capabilities of the user's device and available connectivity.

There also needs to be consideration here for the size and ease of accessing and downloading of web pages regarding packet data, for many mobile service providers charge for the download of packet data and so if your web site is not cross platform compatible, simple and efficient, you may well be landing visitors with huge bills and this is not good for any web site or service. For the harsh reality is, web surfers and potential customers simply will not return!

Cross platform compatibility is the ability in design to meet the needs of all users seeking to access your web site and using any form of device be it a Laptop, Desktop PC, Mobile Phone, Tablet, Smart TV or Netbook etc.

2/. Reduce Content Size

As mentioned above in the previous section we discus cross platform compatibility and this falls nicely in line regarding this section of content size, to help the web user wanting to access and view your web site.

The reduction in content size on every web page and especially the landing pages are critical factors, otherwise potential web user visitors will very often experience connectivity problems leading to timing out (404 message).

You also have to consider today as frequently mentioned in the book the very many different device types and their capabilities in respect of the technology hardware's age and processing ability.

The most optimized and efficient web page in the World is a blank one! It is only when we begin to add material data content does any web page or web site begins to become slower and less efficient.

The golden rules of Sir Isaac Newton's Natural Law concerning Quantum Mechanics is to "evolve and refine" and so the greatest skill today in web design and development is the achievement of an architecturally well laid out correctly technically authored venue medium that can be displayed and presented successfully online.

3/. Optimize Any Images

To help the web user's device and the software process, a web site's web pages need to have optimized images, thus enabling the fastest download of these web pages and therefore also reducing the costs to web user who is charged for data downloads.

In the web site content section we will cover this subject in greater detail and how you can optimize and improve performance of any images.

BROWSER SOFTWARE PERFORMANCE MOFIDICATIONS

Here follows the alterations we can make to help the User's Browser Software regarding performance as part of "The New Internet Super Highway" Virtual World Technology advancements in a different dimension and way of thinking.

1/. Assign a Dedicated IP Address

In the Web Server section we began to cover dedicated IP Addresses when we discussed web hosting options. The assigning of dedicated IP Addresses greatly assist and help browser software as they become recognized addresses resolving to your domain name.

For security and trust reasons dedicated IP Addresses also help bolt on partner third party browser software components such as anti-spam and anti-virus services such as Norton and McAfee that are mostly used today in conjunction with browser software such as Internet Explorer, Fire Fox, Chrome, Safari and Opera to mention a few.

2/. Web Hosting Options

To assist greatly the users Browser Software, web hosting is a major consideration and factor as highlighted already in the web server section. Dedicated, Virtual and Shared hosting all have relevant variations in performance. However many very large hosting providers today of any worth will guarantee connectivity for the web site client, this being you as the webmaster or developer a 99.9% uptime.

However this must not be taken as red, for I have experienced over many years some service providers may promise the world but fail miserably on delivery.

Browser Software rendering engines are similar to search engines for data mining collection and finding correctly assigned IP addresses for a domain name resolving to a web site where these records are stored. This is critical and so the hosting package you acquire has to be up to the task by the service provider.

To ensure the greatest efficiency surrounding this subject area to ensure your web site is reachable by the web user browser software, always relates to the correct configuration in the Name Server Administration Section on the Web Server.

If you are not conversant or familiar with this area of programming please consult an experienced colleague, or the actual hosting service provider.

3/. Assigned Domain Name

Assigned Domain Names have to be programmed correctly for any domain name and web site to become in existence successfully regarding web user Browser Software. The Domain Name needs to be correctly assigned to the IP Addresses on the Web Server. For as we know Computers and Servers talk to each other through the WAN (Wide Area Network) using assigned Name Server IP Addresses and not a domain name. Domain Names are married up as mentioned before in the Name Server Administration section of the Web Server Operating System and Program.

4/. Technically Authored Correctly

Another crucial factor as mentioned in the book and throughout is correct technical authoring, to prevent the delay of any web site or web page. Delays come from poor technical authoring and where the web user's

Browser Software is unable to interpret, or read the content being delivered via requests in packet data form.

WEB SITE PERFORMANCE MODIFICATIONS

Here follows the alterations that can be made regarding Web Site performance modifications as part of "The New Internet Super Highway" Virtual World Technology advancements in a different dimension and way of thinking.

1/. Avoid Character Set in the Meta Tag

This can be confusing to many regarding character sets such as "UTF-8" in a Meta Tag or a HTTP header. I have found developing and using the new standard of HTML 5.0 (RDFa) when encoding into a HTTP Header can deliver coding errors or the failing of W3C compliant standards for Html 5.0.

The following example which I have configured to meet W3C compliant standards is taken from my home page header source code.

Example:

This I have placed in the head of the Html 5.0 document

```
<meta charset="UTF-8">
```

The above code you must have in your Html web pages and one of the main reasons why is that most web servers run Apache and you simply cannot enter and re-configure this web server program without some really serious consequences if you get it wrong.

2/. Specify Image Dimensions

Specifying image dimensions and sizes may seem common sense when it comes to web hosting and web site performance, but believe me there are many areas for improvement and greater efficiency.

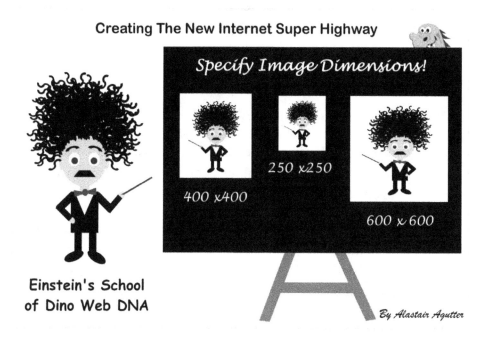

The specification of images in your coding greatly assists web user browser software rendering and ensures the actual images loaded to the web server are of the size required for the web site's web pages. Not over-sized, for then the web users are downloading a far larger image than the one being displayed, therefore taking far longer to deliver and if the user is paying for data downloaded, he or she will not be impressed with your web site venue and will be very reluctant in returning at another time.

Example: If you have an image for example of 1500 x 1500 pixels and require an image of 150 pixels x 150 pixels, make sure you resize the original image to 150 x 150 pixels and save as another file and then upload this new file to the web server, using it in your web page. By resizing and saving as another file, you have created an image file of only 1/10th the size compared to the original image and therefore delivering an image at least 10 times faster in packet data form. I say at least 10 times, for I have mentioned in the book earlier and explained the phenomena and anomalies of how packet data in particle matter form can defy our one dimensional thinking and logic. For as mentioned again and again, Quantum Mechanics can equate too many variables including maths when we study fractals.

3/. Minify Cascading Style Sheets (CSS)

When Cascading Stylesheets are created there are many sections that can be refined. This relates to RGB colour coding abbreviations to omitting certain code instructions that are not required in that particular module.

A Black background colour in RGB coding would equal #000000 and a Dark Navy hyperlink equals #000099. Now these colours can be refined very easily. Black for example can become #000 and the Navy Blue hyperlink colour can become #099.

If you have margins and headers in one web page design module for example and not in others that relate to the CSS coding of a particular web page and the coding elements are just listed with either 0px or 0pt for example, simply remove these instructions from the CSS document.

4/. Minify Java Script if Applicable

The Compact and compressing of Java Script Code again contributes to greater refinement and helps to increase speed and performance. As mentioned earlier, all such elements that can save bytes of packet data size and just like an athlete, always training to find that extra 1% margin in a number of disciplines and when grouped together is the difference between winning or losing.

It is surprising how you can eliminate the byte size of packet data, some examples being; even removing spaces and line breaks from a coding Java Script.

5/. Optimize Images and Formats

Images are very often large Rich Media content packet data elements and therefore do create latency in delivery of any web page and the image or images that are associated.

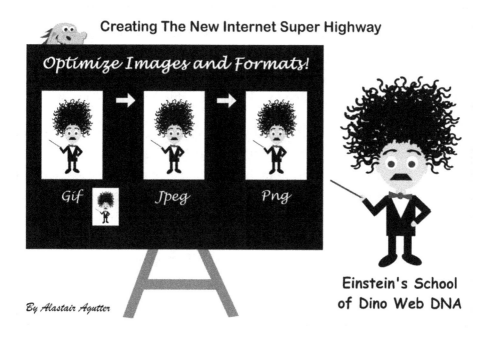

Many images broadly used today across web sites and social media networks are Jpeg's (Joint Photographic Experts Group). However there are many varying options available when using visual packet data more efficiently.

The first being as covered earlier is the actual size of the file image corresponding with the actual web page image presentation. Again this is worth remembering, for example say an average image taken is 2500 pixels by 1000 pixels but the actual web page image to be used is only 250 pixels by 100 pixels, it is wise to edit and re-size such an image and save it as another file. Then the said file created can be uploaded to the web server and used for the web page presentation and at only a fraction of the original size and therefore increasing performance and downloading speed of the packet data regarding the image by at least ten times.

Other options available to increasing speed and performance is by possibly changing the actual format of the image in question. If you have a small image that does not necessarily require high definition the image could be transformed to a Gif (Graphics Interchange Format) file, or if it is an image that is small but does require crystal clear presentation, you could change the format of the image to a PNG (Portable Network Graphic).

There are other ways to increase download speed and efficiency regarding rich media such as graphics by further reducing the size of an image. If you have a really crystal clear high quality image for example say 250 pixels by 250 pixels and this is the size you want presented in the web page. You could in fact reduce the size of the image again by editing to say 200 pixels by 200 pixels so the packet file becomes smaller again but keeping the size of the presentation in the web page at 250 pixels by 250 pixels by stating in your web page coding the actual size of the image.

Here below is a code line from one of my web pages regarding an image and as you can see where I state the size of the image in question. It does not mean the actual image I have uploaded as a packet data file is necessarily the actual size specified, as mentioned it could be say 30% smaller and therefore reducing the packet data size of the image file by a further 1/3rd and as a result further increasing downloading speed of the image and thus in turn the actual web page the web user is accessing to view via their browser software.

Example:

```
<a
 href="http://www.alastairagutter.com/best-sellers/"><img
 alt="Alastair R Agutter Author's Best Selling Books Chart"
 src="http://www.alastairagutter.com/journal-covers/author-
journal-cover-450x310-027.jpg"
 title="Alastair R Agutter Author's Best Selling Books
Chart"
 style="border: 0px solid ; width: 310px; height:
450px;"></a>
```

As you can see from the above example and code it states the actual size of the image. As mentioned if the image is crystal clear and say we wanted to increase this size with the same size image we can do so from the html code, by changing for example the width of 310 pixels to 380 pixels and the height of 450 pixels to 520 pixels.

The packet data size of the above Jpeg image in this example of the code above is 215 kb. If this were a BMP (Bitmap Image File) the size would become 409 kb.

Example: Here below shows variations of the same actual image of 310 pixels x 450 pixels that is present in the code earlier and clearly showing the different packet data sizes in various image formats.

1/. Journal Cover Image 27 in JPEG Format = Packet Size 215 kb

2/. Journal Cover Image 27 in BMP Format = Packet Size 409 kb

3/. Journal Cover Image 27 in GIF Format = Packet Size 112 kb

4/. Journal Cover Image 27 in PNG Format = Packet Size 274 kb

If we do take the JPEG Format image above of 450 pixels x 310 pixels and we reduce the size of the image to 380 pixels high and 262 pixels wide the actual packet data image size is reduced then to 165 kb and therefore reducing the packet data size by a further 20%. But the image in the web page code can still remain the actual size desired and this being 450 pixels by 310 pixels. But from my efficiency changes, I have now an image packet size of only 165 kb as opposed to 215 kb and so the downloading speed of this image will now be increased by at least 20%.

Another consideration is mono images today, for they are becoming more fashionable and so by again changing the colour mode of the image can you further improve the speed and efficiency of packet data downloading times.

Example: Same image as above but showing the packet data size difference between full colour and mono.

1/. Journal Image 27 in COLOUR JPEG Format = Packet Size 215 kb

2/. Journal Image 27 in MONO JPEG Format = Packet Size 96 kb

As you can see again here the packet data of the image has been reduced in size by over 50% and therefore increasing downloading speed to twice as fast.

6/. Minify Html

Reducing the size of Html is also possible and especially with the aid of using CSS (Cascading Style Sheets) to assist in this process.

Below I have provided a simple example regarding the re-occurring coding that takes place with something as simple as text.

```
<big style="font-weight: bold; color: rgb(51, 51,
51);"><span
style="font-family: arial;">Reducing the size of html
coding...</span></big>
```

As you can see from the code above this relates to just a simple line of a few words "Reducing the size of html coding..." and where the size, style and colour of the font becomes quiet a significant coding line and has to be repeated on every occasion throughout the html web page wherever written or inserted. Whereas by using CSS you can instruct a font, style, colour and size in a few lines that can relate to all the text on the html web page in paragraph form for example. We do not have to keep repeating the coding instructions for every line and paragraph throughout the html web page and therefore reducing the size of the html packet data considerably.

Here below is a simple CSS code line for all paragraph text that will relate to all of the content written on the web page in this style and format. As you can see from the example code below, only a few lines of CSS code was required and written.

```
p {
   color: #333;
   font-family: Arial;
   font-weight: normal;
   font-size: 12pt;

}
```

7/. Avoid Bad Requests

Avoiding bad requests can very often relate to hyperlinks to other web pages across your web site resulting in a 404, or 410 web page messages giving a very bad experience for the visiting web user. However bad requests can also relate to the linking of CSS files, Icons and Meta Data feeds in relation to further information or images for software rendering engines.

Below is an example code of a Twitter Feed so an image and description can be displayed when linking to this particular page. There are also open source coding to also aid in the display of content for search engines and other social network sites when posting such as Google+. If these links fail to work, they will be rendered as bad requests and fail the measurement or metric standards required by the platform provider and in some instances with a series of bad requests causing a site's web page to crash or worse still, freezing the web users browser software.

```
<meta name="twitter:card" content="summary">
  <meta name="twitter:site"
content="@AlastairAgutter">
  <meta name="twitter:creator"
content="@AlastairAgutter">
  <meta property="og:url"
content="http://www.alastairagutter.com/">
  <meta property="og:title" content="Alastair Agutter
© Official Site">
  <meta property="og:description"
 content="Alastair R Agutter Amazon Best Selling
Author, Senior Web Developer, Author's Journal for
Specialist Books, Hobbies and Interests.">
  <meta property="og:image"
 content="http://www.alastairagutter.com/journal-
covers/author-journal-cover-450x310-027.jpg">
```

When there are bad requests between the web user browser software and the web server hosting the web site content, seconds and minutes pass as requests are constantly being repeated and made believing such packet data information exists relating to the relevant links.

So as a web site evolves with more web pages, it is always important to double check and to test all forms of links on every page created, to avoid bad requests of any form.

8/. Defer Parsing of Java Script

There are many techniques and methods surrounding the deferring and parsing of Java Script. The simplest method is to defer the loading of Java Script until it is required or to avoid using such scripting and coding as it will cause greater delay with regards to the rendering of the web page in question.

Java Script coding is often used today in advertisements and can cause considerable delay as mentioned and regardless of the positioning of the Java Script on the web page whether at the top or on the bottom, such positioning will not make any difference as the browser software rendering engine will be finding and searching out the script along with other packet data forms as soon as the instruction is made between the web user and the web server hosting the web site in question.

9/. Inline Small CSS

Inline small CSS (Cascading Style Sheets) is where these small amounts of CSS code can be embedded into the html web page file. Therefore only loading one Html web page as opposed to two, these being the Html web page file itself and the CSS coded document.

This may increase the speed of a page slightly, but not always for if you have other codes on the same html file web page such as Java Script, such an exercise would be deemed academic.

Furthermore, with an external CSS coding file you can update and modify, introducing further styles and features and not having to go back to every html web page that carries the inline CSS code.

CSS files are very small and load very fast, but I believed it was worth mentioning this in the book. For today still a number of well-known organizations do apply this method of inline small CSS, but then they have the longevity and resources in place to address such scenarios of change and it is still very often the case that some of the programming is still being carried out by more dated methods of coding and still using CSS 1.0, CSS 2.0 and Html 3.0 even as opposed to Html 4.01, 5.01 and CSS 3.0 to mention just a few.

10/. Minimize Redirects

Redirects can happen for a number of reasons on a web site itself to even a redirect to another URL (Uniform Resource Locator) and these must be avoided at all times.

Redirects cause massive delays and can in fact impact a web site in relation to web rankings, for Search Engines only spider and data mine on a frequent basis, when certain popular web sites frequently update with more new content and posts. However, less frequented web sites are data mined by search and rendering engines on a less frequent basis and can therefore produce results in search engine listings where these web sites and web pages can be out of date and if changes have been made regarding modifications and the decision to create new web pages in a different location. This can result in a listing being displayed in search engine results still with the old hyperlink address and when pressed by search result users a dead link is delivered and a 404 message.

When content is moved to a different location and this has been the case in the past where there is offered up redirect pages. However these pages can be of great frustration to the users and also search engine spiders when data mining. Especially if there is a delay before the redirect works by switching the user or spider to the new and correct location where the new data is held. Search Engine Spiders work on hundredths of seconds and so any delay often results in a search engine spider moving onto another web site and therefore not all the web pages on your web site are spidered leaving less results in search engine data banks, therefore greatly reducing the risk of search engine users being able to find your relevant web site pages for services or products etc.

When redirects relate to URL's there can be many more greater complications as questions begin to be raised by the browser software, security protection software regarding a visiting web user and for data mining search engines if IP Addresses especially change. But more importantly all such forms of redirects cause massive delays to the delivery of packet data and other delays and problems, some briefly covered here that are invisible to the eye or everyday public.

If you are forced to create a page with a hyperlink taking users to another new web page and section. I would suggest providing some explanation and content on the page in question and so the process becomes more of a mere formality.

If the redirect page in question has some content, even just offering some news of the changes and improvements to the service. This then becomes another web page for search engines to spider and grab, rather than just a redirect.

11/. Minimize Request Size

One of the key points to consider is making sure the packet data size remains below 1500 bytes. This being for CSS documents of coding to

Html web pages and others. When data exceeds the size mentioned it then requires a second packet to deliver the packet data in question.

Top Stories and Books

An average web page in packet data form that is comprehensive can be as little as 900 kb which is the average size of my web pages. Above is a picture screen shot of my home page that includes even background images in the design that can be considerable and only 922 kb in size.

The second following image featured, demonstrates the optimization of the web site home page and where it is superfast and showing the high performance results that you can achieve when a web site is designed for "The New Internet Super Highway" in the 21st Century by following this valuable information found within this book.

The more requests you have on a web page the longer it will take to download via the web user's software browser. This can be exampled below is by studying the performance results in the following image and requests.

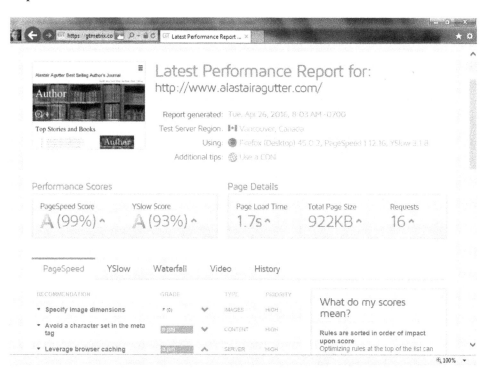

Every request causes delay and if you offer a web site and service that requires high levels of content, by planning out with smart design and correct technical authoring, you can achieve these high performance speeds and standards very easily.

12/. Optimize the Order of Styles and Scripts

If technically authored and planned out with styles and scripts correctly, the process of delivery can be seamless. A web design can be complex and dynamic, but still created by using just HTML and CSS, the coding can link easily in the main Html document.

13/. Put CSS (Cascading Style Sheets) in the Document Head

The putting of CSS coding correctly into an Html document head follows on nicely and I have provided an example below from my web site home page.

This is a scripting code linking to CSS correctly and fully compliant to W3C compliant standards in Html 5.0 and CSS 3.0.

```
<link title="HTML 5 CSS"
 href="http://www.alastairagutter.com/css3/html5-css3-journal-001.css"
 rel="stylesheet" type="text/css">
```

14/. Remove Query Strings from Static Resources

Many web server programs will not process data string queries "?" and so this needs to be avoided regarding any hyperlinks created to other web pages on your site. Such links also cause delay in trying to resolve the connection if a web server program is able to process such a link. In early days of the World Wide Web it was possible to offer up query strings, but with over 94 million web sites today and still counting, it is no longer hit and miss.

15/. Serve Resources from a Consistent URL (Uniform Resource Locator)

If resources are shared across multiple pages ensure in the architecture of the web site a full URL is used and not a local URL or web page address, this is particularly relevant to CSS program files where they serve multiple pages across a web site. Use just one location for the CSS program files and refer to this URL in full, so as the web user explores your web site, further requests are not made for the same program files. This is also relevant for example to logos and other images related to the overall design of the web site we term as a skin.

Then once these files are originally downloaded from the home page or landing page in question there will be no need for further requests of the same files or program script documents, example being CSS program files.

For Mobile device users this is particularly important, especially if they have to pay for data downloads. As they will not appreciate huge unnecessary costs from downloading repeated duplicate file types.

There are also security issues here again if files reside on other servers, or the locations are not necessarily recognized or associated with the consistent URL.

16/. Serve Scaled Images

Server scaled images we covered earlier in the optimization of images, but if you are using on your web pages an image say 200 pixels by 200 pixels, please make sure you upload to the web server an image file related to this section of the web page that is scaled to that exact size to ensure downloading speed and efficiency is maintained.

When oversized images are used, this is the size of the download that the web user has to wait for before the image is visible on the web page in question.

Always remember Rich Media and Third Party Media (advertisements) cause the greatest delays in web site and web page rendering by the web users browser software program and images as they fall into this category.

17/. Avoid CSS (Cascading Style Sheets) @ import

I have covered this earlier really and so I have provided another example link tag to use for CSS programs files so they download fast and simultaneously. Using @import CSS files in a script causes further delay to the web site pages functioning fast and efficiently.

The example below is of a correct linking tag for CSS (Cascading Style Sheets) program files and documents when developing in Html 5.0.

```
<link title="HTML 5 CSS"
 href="http://www.alastairagutter.com/css3/html5-css3-journal-001.css"
 rel="stylesheet" type="text/css">
```

18/. Combine Images by Using CSS Sprites

There is a great deal of literature on the web today with regards to creating image sprites and how by combining a set of images into one and then coding via CSS can you deliver an image presentation from the set at a specified location on the web page.

By using images sprites you can greatly reduce the size of image files from converting them into one, but there can be plusses and minuses surrounding this subject if the coding required becomes just as great as the saving of bytes by merging the images.

When you have small icons in one location such as Social Network buttons and icons and numbers running into 5 or more for example these being Twitter, Facebook, Google Plus, AIM, Stumble Upon, YouTube and Linked-in, you can implement a navigation code with the relevant links. So then the coding is small in the Html body of the document and the image loaded is only one and very small. The image can also be converted from a PNG or Jpeg to a Gif file, making even a greater reduction in size of the image file.

19/. Refer Asynchronous Resources

When a Web Users Browser Software parses a traditional script tag it must wait for the script to download before any html web page is rendered and this can sometimes be evident when visiting some web sites. However, when using an asynchronous the browser can continue to render and parse the Html even when it normally comes after the asynchronous script.

Today Google uses asynchronous analytics JavaScript and this is noticeable in comparison to the past. Sites such as CNN.Com in the past before the new script would take ages to load and all you would initially see for a considerable time was a blank page as the script downloaded before the web pages Html.

So if you are using a Google Analytics script of some age it is worth grabbing a newer version of JavaScript code from Google Webmaster Tools to greatly improve the speed, delivery and performance of the web site.

20/. Third Party Advertisements

Many content web sites today use third party advertisements in their web pages and these can cause massive delays for the rendering and display of a web page to the visiting web user.

Even one such type of advertisement display will delay the delivery of the web page and delaying the download time by a further half. Webmasters using more than one advertisement need to test their web pages with this media, for more ads become academic if users decide to leave your web site as a result of these continued delays. Furthermore such delays cause greater frustration to the web user and in most cases the permanent loss of a new visitor and potential customer if operating a service or ecommerce store.

I do use masses of advertisements on web pages, but only one occasionally when offering free articles, as I am mindful of the delays caused by Web User Browser Software having to go in search of packet data from other sites (third-party) besides the one being visited.

I am not anti-advertising at all and I think some advertisements can complement any web page, especially if there is a mass of text and where the advertisement can actually help break up the monotony of a web page.

However web users with many advertisements on a single web page be warned, as these delays causing difficulty in rendering can result in a Web User's Browser Software hanging or worst still crashing.

This activity today is happening more frequently and across all devices and where some are not that easy to just reload, Smart TV comes to mind.

WEB USER PERFORMANCE MODIFICATIONS

Here follows the alterations we can make to help the Web User regarding performance as part of "The New Internet Super Highway" Virtual World Technology advancements in a different dimension and way of thinking.

1/. Improve Navigation for Users

One of the reasons Html 5.0 has been developed and advanced is to provide a more robust environment across the World Wide Web so to ensure web design complies within a framework that is fast and efficient.

One of my personal bug bears is navigation, where from using mouse over navigation a link appears along with a series of more sub categories. To many in web design this is seen as a "Kool" element in the design of a web site. Yet the reality is it's a feature that causes greater confusion and frustration to the web user. For with great web design there has to be a well thought out plan and with the primary consideration being towards the web user.

Navigation with sub categories even used by the most competent often fails to function correctly, or worse still the web user simply cannot operate such a process.

This to a degree may sound crazy, but I can assure you it is not. I personally as a competent and able web user is very often frustrated when I have to mouse over a category, only to move the mouse to another sub category and all of a sudden it closes before I can execute the hyperlink.

If someone is elderly or frail, this design is completely ridiculous and will cause great frustration to the visiting user and for a simple task of just wanting to link to a particular section of a web site.

Such design can also be difficult for very young users on the web still developing hand co-ordination skills and also members of the community visibly impaired or disabled (Multiple Cerosis, Alzheimer's etc.).

The other key factor to these designs is that they create coding that in most instances fail compliant standards, create more unnecessary coding therefore increasing the packet data size and lastly, reduces the ranking importance of the web page with search engines.

The more visible hyperlinks on a web page referring to other parts of the site commands greater rankings. Search Engines when Data Mining a web site will very often pass on and move to another site as the program is unable to access the hyperlinks in a logical data mining process and method.

Other important factors are the various types of browser software used today, can they read and interpret such superficial novelty designs to which they are and can the hardware device function across such a design environment when we consider the very many different types of devices used today, ranging from PC's, Tablets, Mobiles through to Smart Television, the latter especially.

Great web design keeps things simple so the web user does not even have to think. Remember Steve Jobs philosophy, the objective of getting from A to B and so think like an engineer.

2/. Cross Platform for all Devices

The above leads me onto this section of ensuring a web site is cross platform compatible and here again as mentioned earlier in the book it comes down to risk aversion.

Complex web design is not good, only for the web designer and developers ego. It is certainly not good for the rest of the community in the form of the user, the devices, search engines, browser software the list goes on.

Technical Authoring is the development of the web site architecture and a great designer will ensure the web site is dynamic, clean looking, fast and efficient to enable a seamless experience for the web user thus delivering in turn orders, sales and interest.

A great designer will also test a web site against countless browser software and hardware devices to ensure the web site can be delivered successfully to every device type and user regardless of their location and connectivity. The more complicated a web site becomes, the greater the risk of failure and vast numbers of potential web user visitors across a large geographical landscape spectrum is presented with a far greater risk of being unable to access the web site in question.

Cross platform compatibility does not mean a web site has to look bland. A well designed web site can look stunning and a walk in the park for navigating regarding the most important consideration this being towards your visiting web user.

3/. Optimize Landing Pages

The foundation of this book is to look beyond a one dimensional form of thinking to achieve greater speed and efficiency in a virtual world.

The more we create and add to every single web page increases the packet data size. However again from smart design, web pages can be rich in content, products and information, if a web site is well designed and technically authored correctly, so the process of rendering by the web users browser software is straight forward when packet data requests are made.

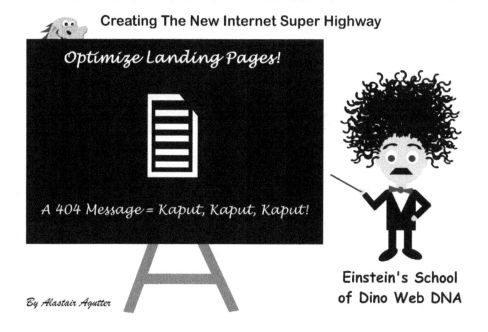

The failure to optimize web pages and especially landing pages in the way of Home, News and Store so often found in search engine results can often mean the dreaded 404 message, if users are from many different parts of the World with varying degrees of connectivity.

So these pages must be optimized and incorporated within this process the "Skin", this being the overall design of the site regarding logos and brand recognition shell schemes. These elements especially should be optimized to the highest standards, for they should be a constant throughout the web site and therefore as a result, should be the first elements to be downloaded along with various other rich media images and text, in the form of written content material relevant to that particular section of the web site.

COMPLIANT HTML VALIDATION

(Hyper-Text Mark-up Language)

When it comes to validated and compliant Html there is no point in diving down behind a chair and hiding, as you await the web site and web page(s) results.

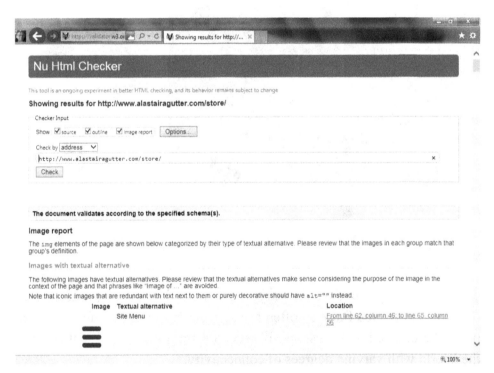

As a webmaster or developer, your ability to deliver compliant standard Html is a very valuable asset in your armoury in a very competitive world and a very "BIG" selling feature, regarding the services you can offer to potential clients.

To aid in this process and to better understand the new coding standards of the Html 5.0 (fifth core element) framework, the World Wide Web Consortium (W3C) provides comprehensive working papers and resources online from www.w3.org to assist all webmasters and developers in these continued current changes as the Html 5.0 framework (RDFa) is still under development since its inception and launch in 2014.

The World Wide Web Consortium (W3C) also provides an Html validation service (https://validator.w3.org/) so web developers and webmasters can check their Html work for coding errors, as these technical authoring mistakes do cause significant delays in rendering web pages through a browser software program.

It is also worth remembering that browser software programming development is forever changing today, as they upgrade browser software bundles and incorporate these new HTML 5.0 (RDFa) framework standards.

I am sure many developers and webmasters fail to realize that technical authoring errors on web pages also relate to the browser software endeavouring to read and interpret such packet data.

When engaging in this process as a webmaster or developer, it can sometimes be daunting when results are produced with errors. But this is more of a reflection on the education system in Computer Sciences surrounding young webmasters and developers today.

These areas of delivering fully compliant and valid Html cannot be emphasized enough when technically authoring. The very reason for more stringent and robust solutions in the HTML 5.0 (RDFa) framework is as a result of poor design, creating the threat of greater chaos and clutter across the World Wide Web.

Meeting these standards will lift any webmaster or developer to new heights in the advancement of Computer Sciences Programming. As developers you will also be starting that road of greater human enlightenment by respecting and applying the rules of Natural Law surrounding Quantum Mechanics to "evolve and refine" that is evident as a constant in all that we see and know.

COMPLIANT CSS VALIDATION

Like Html the ability to technically author and code correctly CSS (Cascading Style Sheets) is a massive plus as a webmaster or developer and will only serve you well now and in the future.

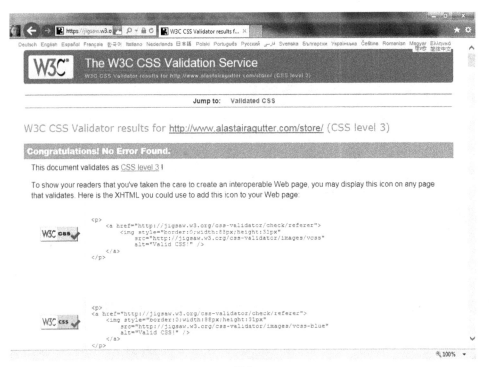

Your ability to code correctly, is also serving to the benefit of your client's web sites and the community by uncluttering the Internet, where currently bad packet data is causing major bottlenecks and congestion to the global community networks.

For webmasters and developers to program and code to validated compliant CSS (Cascading Style Sheets) standards enables the significant reduction in coding. A CSS program coded document can eliminate so many duplicating factors found in HTML and even in CSS documents. Some that come to mind are with reference to text, fonts and formats to margins and spacing's etc.

A CSS (Cascading Style Sheets) correctly coded program document can also serve many web pages at any one time and this allows the browser software to make one request of a packet data file that may relate to several hundred other pages or even tens of thousands in just one hit. This then allows any further viewing by the web user across such a web site correctly technically authored in this way, a superfast experience and well beyond the norms of the current standards of convention (status quo).

We are all accustomed to the word "stealth" today and in the World of Computer Sciences relating to WWW technical authoring by applying this new way of thinking and development, you are in fact creating stealth elements to your programming resulting in stealth web pages and a stealth web site.

The amount of instruction that can be programmed into a CSS coded program document that can be delivered just once instead of thousands of other times is exactly stealth in its most beautiful and simplest efficient form.

CSS offers the ability to determine design and style of a site from layout, fonts, to background schemes etc. There are many possibilities open in this form of programming that is far smaller in packet data size.

Colleagues and friends at the World Wide Web Consortium (WC3) also offer a comprehensive range of informative guides and working papers (https://www.w3.org/Style/CSS/learning) and these are very useful for CSS 3.0 especially, as it continues to advance in this field of development.

The World Wide Web Consortium (W3C) also provides a CSS validation facility for testing your CSS programming and coding by using the following web site address: https://jigsaw.w3.org/css-validator/

Again, do not be daunted by the validation results as this just puts you on the right path for greater enlightenment and serving the community as a webmaster and developer of means, by technically authoring high compliant standard coding and thus in turn helping the World Community at large as we will require more space and storage, plus faster and more efficient connectivity for data especially, concerning advancements in Physics, Science (Hadron Collider Particle Atoms) and Biochemistry (Genetic and Organic Engineering).

Below is an example programming code of how we can embed featured images into CSS today.

```
#media {
background-image:
url(http://www.alastairagutter.com/displays/aa-author-
display-001.jpg);
background-size: cover;
margin-top: 10px;
margin-left: 10px;
margin-right: 10px;
margin-bottom: 10px;
}
```

If you are new to programming and coding of CSS (Cascading Style Sheets) it may seem confusing or overwhelming initially from some examples seen across the web. But there are examples that can be found that are well laid out to help you easily follow and learn.

For further insight to HTML 5.0, CSS 3.0 and RWD (Responsive Web Design). I hope to have released this year the "Creative Web Design Book" for Webmaster and Developer Readers.

QUALITY ASSURANCE STANDARDS

Quality Assurance as a field to many webmasters and developers may seem an unlikely consideration or scenario.

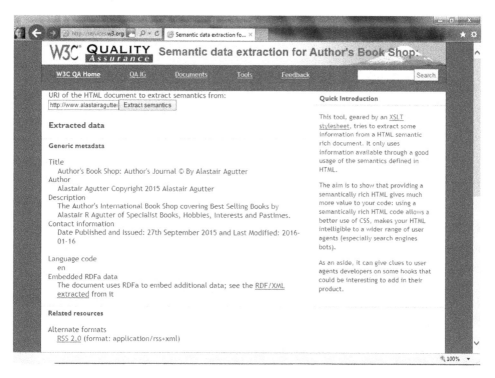

But be rest assured, such standards exist and meeting these again takes your skills and credibility to a whole new level and well beyond the realms of your contemporaries.

For search engines, browser software and security programs measure this information to a very high degree to help assist and establish the structure of the web site and related web pages often referred to as web semantics.

Quality Assurance plays a significant role in all our lives today across many industries and services, with regards to standards surrounding credible and reliable trustworthy services and programming on the World Wide Web in the field of Computer Science is no different.

When a Search Engine is Data Mining a great deal of the information found from running these tests is gathered and used to determine the ranking and content relevance to deliver accurate search results for users.

The same can be said for Browser Software as they gather data in addition to IP Addresses and Domain Names.

Security Program bundles also evaluate such data to determine the authenticity and integrity of a service in the interests of protecting its user.

The World Wide Web Consortium (W3C) provides further information and documentation surrounding this service and features. To test and identify the structure of your web site and web pages can be carried out by using the World Wide Web Consortiums Quality Assurance Semantic Data Extractor at this address: https://www.w3.org/2003/12/semantic-extractor.html

By understanding the points raised above it demonstrates how important it is for this information to be accurate and consistent, to prevent any further delay to the web user when packet data is requested, so the browser software can very quickly render successfully the web site's web page for the viewing web user.

This particular type of testing is also very helpful to ensure information in the head of the web pages is correct and accurate, especially regarding title, description, copyright etc.

The Quality Assurance Semantic Data Extractor also helps to see the cohesive structure layout in technical authoring terms regarding the outline of the web page document.

To reach the highest standards to meet search engine rankings, nothing should be left to chance. So this program greatly helps to view the Meta Data and Tags. This helps to ensure the head content is correct.

GOOGLE MOBILE FRIENDLY STANDARDS

My friends and colleagues at Google for many years have been presented with the great problem of many varying hardware device types (Laptops, Desktop PC's, Netbooks, Tablets, Mobile Phones, Smart TV's etc.) and "How to" provide a comprehensive search engine result service for all.

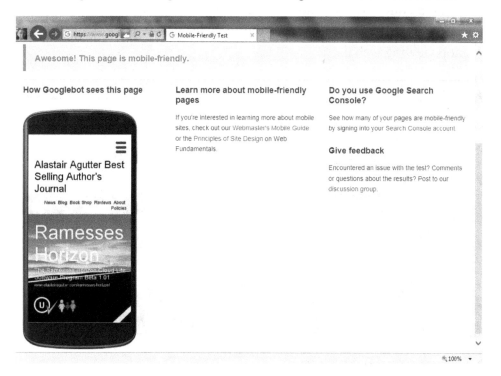

Well that day and time has now arrived, where Google has developed a new metrics algorithm standard we commonly known as "Google Mobile Friendly." For any webmaster, or web site owner, so please take note, for part of the rankings and measurements, consider if your web site accommodates all device types we know of today.

Meeting such standards and also ensuring all coding and programming is compliant and meeting validation standards is no mean feat.

But again these changes demonstrate the advancements being made in this sector of the Computer Sciences sector for it is possible and the image above shows how the dimensions of the Ramesses Horizon Program web pages online have altered dimension to meet the needs of the mobile device user.

Now the picture directly below, shows the same Cloud Program web page altering dimension again to meet the viewing needs of Desktop PC and Laptop viewing web users.

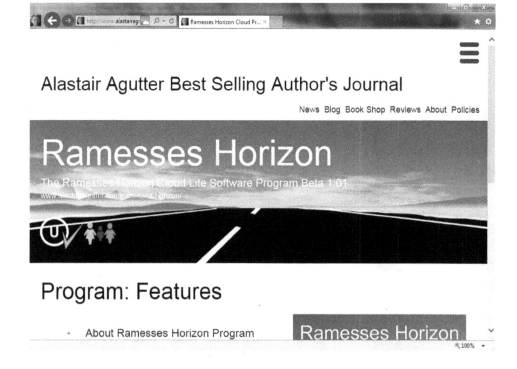

The process and type of "Creative Design" here is known as RWD (Responsive Web Design). This technique alters the dimension of the web site and web pages to meet the web user's device type and if correctly designed as like the examples above, when presented on the device there is now need for magnification or adjustment by the device user.

The download speeds of this design as mentioned earlier is by stealth today, rendering in hundredths of a second and as seen in the following validation speed report where the Ramesses Horizon Program design in HTML 5.0, CSS 3.0 and RWD has loaded in just 856 milliseconds.

As the World becomes forever smaller and more technically advanced I believe it is now the perfect time to start making these critical changes as an Enterprise, Enthusiast, Academic or Service Information community web site owner online.

In many respects the advances discovered and discussed in this book along with the new changes to the web framework in the form of Html 5.0 and the new metrics and algorithms of Google for Mobile Friendly Web Sites, plus the advances of RWD (Responsive Web Design) clearly demonstrates that big things are happening and now is the time to join the New Internet Super Highway.

Throughout history and still even today, the lack of change by some has come at a heavy price.

The Sciences today are gathering momentum as like never before, as more is being discovered regarding our World and beyond each day. The designing and building fast sleek robust systems to carry and store data is becoming therefore forever more apparent and paramount.

Testing of your web site to see if it is Google Mobile Friendly can be done using the following link:

https://www.google.com/webmasters/tools/mobile-friendly/

Again the initial results may seem disappointing and daunting regarding the changes required, but again be rest assured such endeavours made now will deliver better results in the short, medium and long term. Especially if you offer a web development or programming service, where you can capitalize on these new found credible skills.

WEBMASTER TESTING TOOLS

Since my Eureka moment back in 2013 regarding the "flat packing" of the World Wide Web as I call it, to create and invent "The New Internet Super Highway" in a virtual world, a great deal has changed for the greater good.

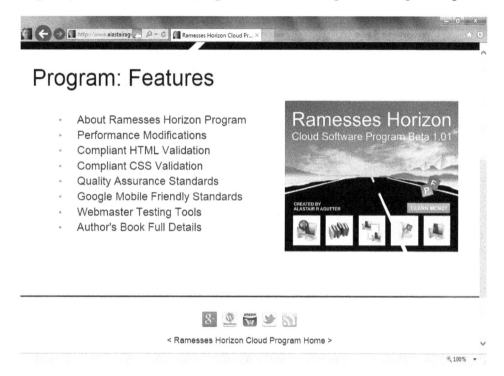

Thankfully today to help the community, there are now many more friends and colleagues sharing my concerns and offering free tools for webmasters, programmers and developers.

So please find the following tools, listing their details with web links, to help towards transforming any web site, so it can join "The New Internet Super Highway" in a virtual world.

At the time of publishing this book, the webmaster tools and web links listed below were current and up to date. Thank You!

1/. Google Analytics

The first thing you will want to do is measure your progress as you make the necessary changes to your web site and web pages. So I recommend joining Google Analytics where you will receive a JavaScript code that can be placed in your web pages to help you identify the geographical location of your web user visitors and the increased traffic. There are also many more features in the program for dissecting valuable data and gaining further insight.

https://www.google.com/analytics/

2/. Google Webmasters

With Google Webmasters you can track the performance of your web site with the Google Search Console. The program also includes many more features such as the identification of dead or faulty hyperlinks.

https://www.google.com/webmasters/

3/. Google Mobile Friendly Testing Tool

As mentioned a web site today has to cater for every device type and the Google Mobile Friendly Tool will test your web pages to see if your work is cross platform compatible.

https://www.google.com/webmasters/tools/mobile-friendly/

Continued....

4/. W3C Html Validator

Html we know is key to any web site and web page created, this testing tool from W3C will ensure your technical authoring is correct and meeting compliant standards, to ensure fast rendering of your creations through a user's browser software.

https://validator.w3.org/

5/. W3C CSS Validator

The CSS Validator from W3C allows us to check our Cascading Style Sheets to ensure they meet compliant standards to aid the delivery of web sites and web pages smoothly and without any unnecessary delays from poor technical authoring.

https://jigsaw.w3.org/css-validator/

6/. W3C RSS Validator

I have listed the W3C RSS (Really Simple Syndication) Validator for we very rarely consider this elements performance and RSS Feeds can be very powerful mediums reaching users in live time via their browser software and so any errors or delays need to be eradicated.

https://validator.w3.org/feed/

7/. Microsoft MSDN

For nearly 20 years I have used and been a member of MSDN and it is an invaluable venue for resources when developing web sites and keeping up to date with the many changes and advancements in our industry.

https://msdn.microsoft.com/en-gb/

8/. Microsoft TechNet

Microsoft TechNet is another invaluable resource for IT professionals providing numerous tools, software and information to further advance your knowledge and skills.

https://technet.microsoft.com/en-gb/

9/. Google Page Speed Insights

This tools tests the performance speed of your web site and within the program you will receive a breakdown of data including your web site and web pages bounce rate which is a critical measurement to determine how many web traffic users are unable to reach you.

https://developers.**google**.com/speed/pagespeed/insights/

10/. Google Chrome Developer Tools

The Google Chrome developer tool allows you to test and view your web site and web pages for desktop and mobile device and details your code lines if corrections or improvements are required.

https://developers.google.com/web/tools/chrome-devtools/iterate/device-mode/?hl=en

11/. Minify CSS Tool

If you are still learning about Cascading Style Sheets and seek help in optimizing and minifying your CSS this tool is perfect for the job and soon helps you become familiar with the changes you can make yourself to your code when technically authoring.

https://cssminifier.com/

12/. Gimp Photo Editing Tool

When it comes to editing and enhancing images the Gimp Software is just the ticket and better still like all tools and software mentioned here it comes free. It will take a while to become familiar with the software, but it is very worthwhile in the long run. A special note regarding this software when wanting to save a file say in Jpeg or PNG for example use "Export As" this will retain the same format of the file you are seeking to alter.

https://www.gimp.org/

13/. Open Office Draw.

Most of my web development life I have used Corel Draw, but after the continuous changes to the software and obscene prices of the product I looked for an alternative. For like me, I know there are many folk who work very hard and believe in value for money when it comes to getting the most from their hard earned cash and so I decided to try "Open Office Draw" and again it comes free. It will take several months to possibly learn all the features, for they do exist and it is just a question of finding the tools on the software.

https://www.openoffice.org/product/draw.html

14/. Image Sprites Tool

In my book "Creative Web Design" I go into a plethora of information and techniques to develop great cross platform compliant web sites, but I have found a tool claiming to help in developing and creating image sprites. I thought this was worth mentioning as we have covered with topic briefly regarding further optimization of rich media.

http://spritegen.website-performance.org/

15/. GT Metrix Speed Testing Tool

As you develop and optimize your web site you will need a guide regarding your progress. GT Metrix provides a free testing service to help you on your way as you continue to fine tune to join the new internet super highway. One special note of caution when developing in HTML 5.0 please remember Html 5.0 is still in development and making many great strides a head for the community and some of the suggestions in GT Metrix is not necessarily up to speed regarding this technology.

https://gtmetrix.com/

16/. Google Chrome Browser

Google Chrome will become an essential tool in your web development when testing your web site across different browser software types to ensure your web site is cross platform compliant and renders correctly.

https://www.google.com/chrome/

17/. Internet Explorer Browser

Internet Explorer is another Browser Software you will need for testing your web site and web pages to ensure they are cross platform compliant.

http://windows.microsoft.com/en-gb/internet-explorer/download-ie

18/. Mozilla Fire Fox Browser

Mozilla Fire Fox is also another Browser Software you will need for testing your web site and web pages to ensure they are cross platform compliant.

https://www.mozilla.org/en-GB/firefox/

19/. Opera Browser

Opera is also another Browser Software you will need for testing your web site and web pages to ensure they are cross platform compliant. This software is more known for mobile and tablet devices these days but has always been a very fast and reliable browser bundle that many folk use world-wide.

http://www.opera.com/

20/. Apple Safari Browser

Apple Safari is also another Browser Software you will need for testing your web site and web pages to ensure they are cross platform compliant. It is also worth remembering that Safari along with Mozilla Firefox now offers many new features for HTML 5.0 including "Reader" for web users and so ensuring your web site is technically authored correctly enables these features to be used. Please see example below where Fire Fox has opened the Reader feature from one of my web site pages.

http://www.apple.com/uk/safari/

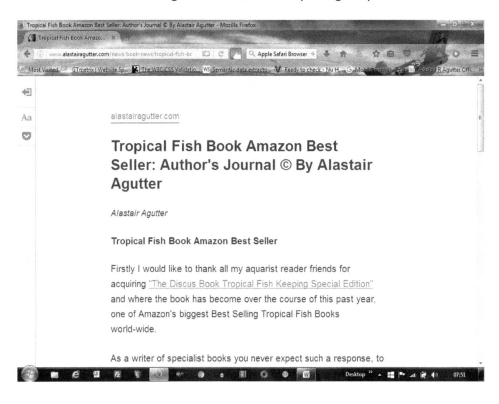

21/. Sea Monkey Web Site Editor

Sea Monkey is a descendent of the famous Netscape Browser Suite Software bundle and was an invaluable tool for all folk starting out in web site design many years ago. The program allowed you to see what you were creating known as "WYSIWYG" (What You See Is What You Get). So I have included this in the book, as it is very important to me to help and encourage our young members in society to develop and become engaged.

http://www.seamonkey-project.org/

22/. World Parental Ratings Certificates Program

As early as 1998 I started to mull over ideas and concerns regarding web safety and etiquette. In 2006 I created the Parental Ratings and Certificates Program and initially developed this with friends and colleagues at the Mozilla Development Foundation using their servers and the project was known as "Mozeditor" to help provide a self-policing program and set of free tools to protect minors and other vulnerable members of society online. Today web developers and programmers can grab the related certificates free for their web sites to further enhance rankings and ethical standards of their web sites online for the good of the community.

http://www.alastairagutter.com/world-parental-ratings/

ACKNOWLEDGEMENTS

For more than 22 years as a professional programmer and senior developer on the World Wide Web. I have had the great privilege and opportunity to work and partner with many of the very best in our industry on projects to shape and make a better world for all.

So special thanks goes out to my friends and colleagues at Microsoft, Google, Amazon, Mozilla, IBM, The World Wide Web Consortium (W3C), Apple, AOL and many others.

AUTHOR'S NOTES AND COMMENTS

Firstly, I would like to truly thank you for acquiring this book and secondly, share with you some of my personal thoughts, observations and comments surrounding this subject and looking into the future.

I know some parts of the book may have seemed hard going at times and speaking personally it has also been very tough going writing on the subject, a mammoth task in fact, trying to relay and articulate my findings and how it all falls into the grand scheme of things or the big soup as I call it regarding us, all life, everything we currently know and beyond as we look out into the dark night of the Cosmos we seek to explore to gain further knowledge.

Some may be sceptical regarding my findings and how I predict things will change. So I remind ourselves all again that the Computers used in the successful Apollo Moon landings in the 1960's can now be the size of our thumbnail and the computers we know of today can store the entire works of the British Library on them.

I know if the book is read again, or frequently referred too, as time and development moves on, I know my readers will also be able to share in my eureka moments, as they further advance and begin to see how the pieces of the jigsaw all begin to fit and see before their very own eyes the dramatic changes and positive results from their endeavours.

When I had to start coding in CSS, it did take me a couple of years before I could describe myself as able and confident. So things do not happen overnight and the realms of Natural Law, Quantum Mechanics and Natural Branching, teaches us that there is no time, only the question of getting it right, as the journey of all evolution continues.

At this time in the Human Race Story and Journey this is the most critical and challenging period for whilst technology is becoming a friend to many, many are also in fear of change and these advances. The common denominator to such human behaviour relates to the most precious and priceless gift of all and this being knowledge through education.

The events across the Middle East at this time in relation to conflict, relates to primitives doctrines of the past and tribalism. Many through fear hold onto such backward doctrines and ideology today for fear of change and a lack of education.

Human evolution and advancement has always derived from the power of thought, this we see through the ages in the form of art, poetry and music etc. Such moments in the history of humanity has provided the beginning of civilized world's, yet sadly often lost from eventual conflict for the desire of possession and greed.

Such ideologies in the coming years cannot be allowed to be present for if they are future destruction will lead to the extinction of the human race and many other life forms we have had the privilege to come to love and know.

As programmers and developers in the World of Computer Sciences the weighted burden on each and every individual's shoulders can never be measured in any form. Today from the Computer Sciences it has allowed the human race to explore deeper into the Cosmos and the World of organic life forms we know and call bio-chemistry. This such period in the human journey is where computer science begins the journey of new life forms, some will say "playing God" and so I hope such a saying or statement helps to understand the gravity of all that we do now and moving forward in the very near future.

Human extinction at this time is not a possibility but a probability unless the Sciences and the World of Academia win the day in our global society. Corporate Industrialization today is leading to the same outcome of the Dinosaurs before the day of destruction regarding a comet, meteor or asteroid some 65 million years ago for as a result of life form impact upon the planet then and as a result the atmosphere began to change and where many specie forms became extinct.

275 is a number we should all know, for it relates to the parts per million of Carbon Dioxide (Co2) for the beginning of all life forms we know including the human race.

Today like the Dinosaurs the atmosphere is now changing again dramatically from Corporate Industrialization and where Carbon Dioxide levels have now gone past the 400 parts per million levels and within a matter of a handful of years will have doubled.

Like the Dinosaurs such atmospheric changes lead to the impact on species leading to extinction. Today we have already lost in the last 50 years 1/3rd of the World's animal, insect and plant life forms.

Today also we are seeing the emergence of new more deadlier and prevalent diseases as a result of climate change including Microcephaly where the human brain is much smaller in size. We are also seeing more record cases of Alzheimer's, a cell deterioration to the brain and again directly related to industrial pollution for the air taken in by any human to fuel brain growth and development in the form of cell regeneration from oxygen is now heavily polluted from toxics such as Carbon and Nitrogen Dioxide.

To advance further and safely by respecting Natural Law, the human race has to learn to co-exist with all life forms and to maintain. It is our responsibility to ensure we create such an environment and society here on Earth before we begin to explore and colonize other parts of this Universe. For failing to respect such a covenant set down in Natural Law we as a species will become another extinction statistic.

Even if this book gives you time for thought, it has served its purpose as a webmaster, developer or interested party. For I hope from the power of thought it has released you from the confines of the status quo and one dimensional thinking.

Today the Science community are trying to tackle Space Exploration in earnest and especially space travel! Nearly 100 years ago Serbian Scientist Nicola Tesla was very often ridiculed and even accused of being mad. But this was far from the truth, for increased genius comes with that a burden and a withdrawal more from society, for as one further enlightens oneself you find little time for the mundane and superficial fodder so often spoken.

One such area of work by Tesla the "Genius" was in the belief electro-magnetic pulse was possible and now today such outlandish views held then nearly 100 years ago, are now being confirmed and realized, after recent LIGO (Laser Interferometer Gravitational-Wave Observatory) results detecting gravitational waves throughout the cosmos and the further confirmation of the existence of dark matter or dark energy today.

So as you embark on these changes to create faster web sites in a virtual world, just remember all and everything is possible, that's a fact for that is precisely how Natural Law and Quantum Mechanics works constantly evolving and refining with work arounds if need be.

Like Albert Einstein, I have no time for the establishment and as Albert once said, "I am right and they are all wrong and will go away". Well dear friends, there by the grace of God go I!

So let's work together in the advancement of the human story and all other life forms for the greater good!

Peace, Love and Sincere Best Wishes for the Future,

Alastair R Agutter

AUTHOR'S OTHER PUBLICATIONS

I dedicate my life these days to writing many specialist books to help contribute in a humble way to advance the human journey and story. So for my readers of this book and particular field of interest, I have listed below some of my other publications I have written over the years that maybe of interest and are all related in some way. Thank You.

1/. Creating The New Internet Super Highway

This is of course the book you have just read and I sincerely hope you have found the publication inspiring to be part of the new human journey and story as it unfolds.

http://www.alastairagutter.com/book-reviews/creating-the-internet-super-highway/

2/. Getting Inside Google's Head Business Edition

Getting Inside Google's Head is a book dedicated to ensuring the fundamentals are in place that are the most critical for success online with search engines by ensuring the Meta Data is coherent and web pages are named correctly to form a logical and effective architecture for search and browser engines to successfully grab your web site's details for all web users world-wide.

http://www.alastairagutter.com/book-reviews/getting-inside-googles-head-business-economy-edition-book/

3/. Creative Web Design

Creative Web Design is a comprehensive book covering philosophy of design through to the correct methods and coding of technical authoring. The book is laid out in a course work format for Web Developers, Business IT Programmers and Members of the Education system teaching Html 5.0, CSS 3.0, RWD, Data Visualization and more.

http://www.alastairagutter.com/book-reviews/creative-web-design/

4/. The Five Minute Guide to HTML 5.0

The indication to this book is in the title and is a quick guide for any Business, Agency or Education system seeking to get up to speed regarding Html 5.0 and in need for some rapid insight to Html 5.0 regarding the dynamic changes underway and the many features this new fifth core element offers.

http://www.alastairagutter.com/book-reviews/the-five-minute-guide-to-html-5-book/

5/. The Theory of Particle Matter Frequencies and Multiple Universes

This may seem initially as an unusual book to have featured here in a Computer Science publication. However, I can assure readers all is relevant as we begin to further understand how "The Big Soup" functions and evolves for there is far more beyond the canvas that any of us can see.

http://www.alastairagutter.com/book-reviews/the-theory-of-particle-matter-frequencies-and-multiple-universes/

6/. Getting Inside Google's Head Colour Edition

This edition of Getting Inside Google's head is a full colour collectors version for the great enthusiasts fascinated with web design, technology and all things geek to keep and enjoy.

http://www.alastairagutter.com/book-reviews/getting-inside-googles-head-book/

7/. A Celebration of Web Art

For over 30 years I have been involved with creative design professionally and this book covers a small collection of creative digital art I have created spanning over 20 years from the early days of the web to the current day. A time capsule showing the limitations in the early days of the web for creative design to the more dynamic illustrations and images of today produced in 32 bit colour.

http://www.alastairagutter.com/book-reviews/a-book-for-celebrating-web-art/

8/ The Reality of Climate Change

I have often mentioned through the book the great burden that befalls the programmer and developer today. This book the Reality of Climate Change is particularly pertinent for it may only be from technology can we save the day regarding all life on Earth. This book provides detailed events happening now to wild life, plants and atmosphere causing many modern day health problems including respiratory disorders and Alzheimer's.

http://www.alastairagutter.com/book-reviews/the-reality-of-climate-change-book/

9/. Gardening For Beginners Book

I have featured this book and subject as it has been my saving grace over the years for creating balance in one's life and by studying the mechanics of nature and life up close, can such discoveries provide so many logical answers that will help towards better work practices and being more creative, looking beyond the confines of the status quo.

http://www.alastairagutter.com/book-reviews/gardening-for-beginners/

10/. Social Media The Sum of Everything Equals Zero Book

The cracks are now beginning to be exposed regarding the World of Social Media. In fact many who engage still do not fully understand how to get Social Media working for them. This book provides frank and honest insight including the history and birth of Social Media through to Marketing, Health, Legal and the eventual winners in this particular technology race.

http://www.alastairagutter.com/news/book-news/social-media-the-sum-of-everything-equals-zero-new-book-release.php

Author's Official Web Site

The Author's Official Web Site provides a comprehensive and entire listing of all specialist books written to inspire and help as reference. Thank You!

http://www.alastairagutter.com/

Availability:

The New Internet Super Highway Book is available online and world-wide from all good book stores.

The formats available for readers to purchase are the traditional printed form and also Digital Editions.

This book is also available through the wholesale Expanded Distribution Network for Libraries, Academia, Retailers and Book Stores.

Copyright Rules

News and Updates

The Author can be reached on Twitter for the latest news and updates.

https://twitter.com/AlastairAgutter

@AlastairAgutter

www.ingramcontent.com/pod-product-compliance
Lightning Source LLC
Chambersburg PA
CBHW071205050326
40689CB00011B/2245